MEETING JESUS AND FOLLOWING HIM

FRANCIS CARDINAL ARINZE

Meeting Jesus and Following Him

*A Retreat Given
to Pope Benedict XVI
and the Papal Household*

IGNATIUS PRESS   SAN FRANCISCO

Cover art:
Christ and the Apostles Sailing on Lake Gennesaret
Cristoforo De Predis (1440–1486)
Biblioteca Reale, Turin, Italy
© Alinari/Art Resources, New York

Cover design by Roxanne Mei Lum

© 2010 by Ignatius Press, San Francisco
All rights reserved
ISBN 978-1-58617-423-1
Library of Congress Control Number 2009935084
Printed in the United States of America ∞

CONTENTS

I

INTRODUCTION

"Follow me" (Mt 4:19; Mk 1:17; Lk 5:27; Jn 1:43). These are engaging and essential words that our beloved Lord Jesus Christ addressed to some of his first disciples. And "they stayed with him that day" (Jn 1:39). This program will guide our meditations during these six days.

As you might guess, it was not without surprise and even fear that I received from the Holy Father the assignment to propose to you these meditations. My first temptation was to react like the prophet Jeremiah at the beginning of his call: "Ah, Lord GOD! Behold, I do not know how to speak, for I am only a youth." The prophet continues: "But the LORD said to me, 'Do not say, "I am only a youth"; for to all to whom I send you you shall go, and whatever I command you you shall speak'" (Jer 1:6–7).

But the following considerations came to my mind. This choice, this decision, comes from the Vicar of Christ. What other sign do you want to know the will of God? Moreover, the person who proposes the meditations for such spiritual exercises should strive to propose, not his own ideas or opinions, but what he believes to be the will of God, the word of the Lord. It is the Holy Spirit that animates retreats and illumines hearts, while the preacher is only an instrument. I am reassured also by the thought that you have come, not to listen to a learned professor who lectures, but to share some experiences and convictions of one who has tried to serve the Lord in the priesthood for half a century, the first half as a diocesan priest and bishop, and the other half in the Roman Curia. I shall therefore try to forget myself and concentrate on these experiences and convictions.

1. *The Priest*

The red thread that will run through all of these meditations is the image of the priest, who, called by Jesus, meets him, follows him, and seeks each day to become a better disciple. " 'What do you seek?' And they said to him, 'Rabbi, where are you staying?' He said to them, 'Come and see.' They came and saw where he was staying; and they stayed with him that day" (Jn 1:38–39). These first disciples, who later became the first Apostles and the first priests, stayed with Jesus not only that day but right up to the day of the Ascension of Christ into heaven, that is, throughout his public life.

In these meditations, the word *priest* will be used. It will generally include all those who have received the ministerial priesthood in the Church, from the young presbyter just ordained to older priests, to bishops and also cardinals, and to the Holy Father. The context will indicate the distinction that is to be made.

The priesthood of Jesus Christ is one. It is manifested in a visibly moving way on Holy Thursday in the Papal Basilica of Saint Peter when the Holy Father concelebrates with a very large number of his priests of the Roman clergy and with cardinals, bishops, and other priests of the Roman Curia. In that solemn Chrism Mass all these priests of Christ renew their priestly promises. Every diocesan bishop concelebrates with his clergy in his cathedral church, and at the end of the rite he turns to the people and asks for their prayers so that he may become every day an image ever more perfect of Christ the Priest, the Good Shepherd, the Teacher and the Servant of all.[1] When, therefore, the word *priest* is mentioned in the following meditations, there is no intention of ignoring the hierarchical order in the participation in the one priesthood of Christ.

Here is a simple illustration. As I stepped out of the Vatican basilica after solemn Vespers on December 31 last year [2008], a young priest saw the cardinal red and, with joy on his face, greeted me, saying: "Best wishes for the new year, Your Eminence; I am a priest." My reply was not long in coming: "I also am a priest. Best wishes for the new year about to begin." And we exchanged smiles of peace and joy in the priesthood of Christ!

2. *The Priest,* Alter Christus

These meditations will consider the priest as a disciple of Christ. It is Jesus who takes the initiative and calls him. It is Jesus who gives him the correct direction for his life. It is Jesus whom he should follow and imitate.

But there is also the dimension of the priest being a minister. Through presbyteral ordination, the Holy Spirit renders the priest capable of acting in the Person of Christ the Head for the service of all the members of the Church.[2] "In the ecclesial service of the ordained minister, it is Christ himself who is present to his Church as Head of his Body, Shepherd

---

[1] Cf. *Roman Missal,* Chrism Mass, 9.

[2] Cf. *Catechism of the Catholic Church,* 2nd ed. (Citta del Vaticano: Libreria Editrice Vaticana, 1997), 1442 (hereafter cited as *CCC*).

of his flock, high priest of the redemptive sacrifice, Teacher of Truth. That is what the Church means by saying that the priest, by virtue of the sacrament of Holy Orders, acts *in persona Christi Capitis*."[3]

The priest is *alter Christus*; he takes the place of Christ. As a consequence of this sacramental reality, to follow Jesus and to be his disciple becomes more urgent. Because of this, the priest has the obligation to follow Jesus even more closely than the other baptized.

3. Overview of These Meditations

For every human being, for every Christian, and even more for every priest, Jesus Christ gives meaning to life. He gives a sense of unity to all the things in which we are engaged. Jesus indicates the correct direction for our life because he is the way, the truth, and the life (cf. Jn 14:6). In these meditations, we shall have in front of us the priest who meets Jesus and follows him.

On the first day, tomorrow [chapters 2–4], we shall meditate on how the priest learns from Jesus to put God in first place. Therefore the priest seeks, with the grace of God, not to permit sin to enter into his life, and to do penance because of his weaknesses.

On Tuesday [chapters 5–7] we will fix attention on the priest who meditates on the mystery of the Incarnate Word and of Christ, the one and only Savior of all. He thanks Jesus, whom he meets in Holy Scripture.

On Wednesday [chapters 8–10] we will concentrate on the gift of Christ that is the Church, his Mystical Body,

[3] *CCC* 1548.

which the priest has the joy to love and serve and in which he has the vocation to evangelize in a dynamic way.

On Thursday [chapters 11–13] we will see the priest at prayer, at the celebration of the sacred liturgy and especially of the Most Holy Eucharist, in the Liturgy of the Hours, and while blessing or using sacramentals, all the time acting as an instrument of Christ and a minister of the Church.

On Friday [chapters 14–16] we will turn the reflections to some instances of justice, peace, and solidarity—or the lack thereof—together with what is expected of the voice of the Church. All will be entrusted to the hands of the Mother of Christ, the eternal High Priest, because she tells us: "Do whatever he tells you" (Jn 2:5).

We shall conclude on Saturday morning [chapter 17] by considering that there is "a time to be born, and a time to die" (Eccles 3:2).

4. Retreat Discipline

As we all know, spiritual exercises do demand from us considerable discipline. Saint Paul, in the short Scripture Reading of Vespers this evening, speaks to us about athletes in sport competitions: "In a race all the runners compete, but only one receives the prize. So run that you may obtain it. Every athlete exercises self-control in all things. They do it to receive a perishable wreath, but we an imperishable" (1 Cor 9:24–25).

During the retreat, we can and should all run, with this difference, that all of us can win the prize. No doubt, we can do it only with the grace of God; as Saint Augustine says, since it is grace that effects in us all our good and meritable works, when God crowns our merits he is only crowning his gifts.[4] The *Roman Missal*, in the first Preface for Saints, sings: "Your glory shines forth in the festive assembly of the Saints, and their triumph celebrates the gifts of your mercy."[5] Saint Paul insists to the Philippians: "Work out your own salvation with fear and trembling; for God is at work in you, both to will and to work for his good pleasure" (Phil 2:12–13).[6] The Council of Trent teaches that the merits of our good works are gifts of the divine goodness.[7] We should therefore place our hope and trust in God's grace.

We entrust these spiritual exercises to the maternal intercession of the Most Blessed Virgin Mary. From her we shall learn how to meet and follow Christ, whom we now adore in the Most Blessed Sacrament of the Altar.

---

[4] Cf. *De gratia et predestinatione*, ep. 154, 5–16; also *Enarrationes in Psalmos*, Ps 102:7.

[5] Cf. also *CCC* 2006–11.

[6] Cf. short reading at Vespers on Wednesday of the First Week of Lent (Phil 2:12–15).

[7] Cf. Heinrich Denzinger and Adolf Schönmetzer, eds., *Enchiridion symbolorum, definitionum et declarationum de rebus fidei et morum*, 1548 (hereafter cited as DS); *CCC* 2010.

II

TRANSCENDENT GOD

God, "the blessed and only Sovereign, the King of kings and Lord of lords, who alone has immortality and dwells in unapproachable light" (1 Tim 6:15–16), "him only shall you serve" (Mt 4:10; cf. Deut 6:13).

1. We Are Created for God

The Psalms and many liturgical texts continue to remind us that we are created by God and for God. "It is he that made us, and we are his; we are his people, and the sheep of his pasture" (Ps 100:3). The first question in the *Compendium of the Catechism of the Catholic Church* puts before us this fundamental truth, God's design for man: "God, infinitely perfect and blessed in himself, in a plan of sheer goodness freely created man to make him share in his own blessed life. In the fullness of time, God the Father sent his Son as the Redeemer and Savior of mankind, fallen into sin, thus calling all into his Church and, through the work of the Holy Spirit, making them adopted children and heirs of his eternal happiness."[1]

In Christ, Saint Paul tells the Ephesians, "according to

[1] *Compendium of the Catechism of the Catholic Church* (Washington, D.C.: United States Conference of Catholic Bishops, 2006).

the purpose of him who accomplishes all things according to the counsel of his will, we who first hoped in Christ have been destined and appointed to live for the praise of his glory" (Eph 1:11–12).

Saint Augustine, after having made the big mistake in his youth of pursuing creatures, finally discovered the fundamental truth, that God created us for himself and that our hearts remain restless until they rest in him.[2] This great Saint of Hippo cries out:

> Late have I loved you, O Beauty ever ancient, ever new, late have I loved you! You were within me, but I was outside, and it was there that I searched for you. In my unloveliness I plunged into the lovely things which you created. You were with me, but I was not with you. Created things kept me from you; yet if they had not been in you they would not have been at all. You called, you shouted, and you broke through my deafness. You flashed, you shone, and you dispelled my blindness. You breathed your fragrance on me; I drew in breath and now I pant for you. I have tasted you, now I hunger and thirst for more. You touched me, and I burned for your peace.[3]

2. Creatures Cannot Give Us Permanent Happiness

No creature can satisfy us in a permanent way because we were not created to find lasting happiness in any creature. Saint John admonishes us: "Do not love the world or the things in the world. If any one loves the world, love for the Father is not in him. For all that is in the world, the lust of the flesh and the lust of the eyes and the pride of life, is not of the Father but is of the world. And the world passes

[2] Cf. *Confessions* 1.1.
[3] Ibid., 10.27.

away, and the lust of it; but he who does the will of God abides forever" (1 Jn 2:15-17).

Pleasure, possessions, and power: that is the sum total of all that the human heart can desire in this valley of tears. These three things, good in themselves, also lead to sin when they are pursued against the will of God. Therefore the immoderate pursuit of pleasure, possessions, and power is also the summary of all the sins that people can commit. When so sought, they are also the compendium of all the errors concerning the reason for human existence, concerning what can procure us permanent happiness.

Solomon had everything he could desire in terms of pleasure, possessions, and power. And yet not only did he not attain lasting happiness, but he lapsed into idolatry (cf. 1 Kings 11:1-13); he called it all "vanity of vanities" (Eccles 1:2), and Sirach (Ecclesiasticus) reserves a harsh judgment for him (cf. Sir 47:19-21).

The sacred liturgy begs God to teach us "to judge wisely the things of earth and to love the things of heaven".[4] In the Prayer after Communion on Monday of the same week, the Church prays the Lord that participation in the sacrament of the Eucharist, which reveals to us pilgrims on earth a Christian meaning to life, may support our steps and guide us to the things of eternity.

3. Consecration to God

The entire Christian life is about consecration to God. The initial consecration is done at Baptism, when we are incorporated into Christ and the Church. It is strengthened in

---

[4] *Roman Missal*, Prayer after Communion, Friday of the First Week of Advent.

Confirmation. It is frequently nourished in the Holy Eucharist. For the service of the Christian people, the sacrament of Holy Orders consecrates deacons, presbyters, and bishops. The rite of religious profession sets men and women apart for God in the consecrated state.

The priest should be the number one person to announce the supremacy of God and the importance of the consecration of persons to God in the states of life just mentioned. We belong to God and not to ourselves. This is true for every human being, and more so for every Christian. But it applies in a yet more demanding way to the bishop, the presbyter, the deacon, and the consecrated person in the religious state or in a society of apostolic life. The Christian people are right when they want to see in these brothers and sisters models of the Christian idea of consecration to God. It is also normal that each of these persons dresses in a way that distinguishes his vocation. From the way they dress we can in fact tell who is a scout, who is a ticket officer on the train, who is a nurse, who is a police officer, even who is a flight attendant of Alitalia, who does not wear the dress of the flight attendant of Lufthansa! Is it not therefore normal that we should be able to distinguish, from the way they vest, who is a bishop, who is a presbyter, and who is a religious sister? Since we are body and spirit, we need visible signs of our consecration to God.

4. Directing the Whole Attention toward God

A consequence of this discipleship, of the Christian life as consecration to God, is the will to direct all our attention toward God. All along in the Gospels, Jesus shows us how to turn to the Father. He did this when he fasted and prayed in the desert; on the mountain, when he praised the Father for having hidden the secrets of the Kingdom from the wise and the learned while revealing them to the little ones (cf. Mt 11:25–27; Lk 10:21–22); when he prayed on the Mount of Olives that not his will but that of the Father be done (cf. Lk 22:42); and when on the Cross he consigned his spirit into the hands of the Father (cf. Lk 23:46).

Let us learn from Jesus to direct our entire life toward God.

5. The Priest, Prophet of the Transcendent God

The priest, by his whole life, should be a silent, and sometimes not so silent, reminder to everyone that God exists, that God is Creator, and that we are his creatures. "Know that the LORD is God! It is he that made us, and we are his; we are his people, and the sheep of his pasture" (Ps 100:3). To God the Creator we owe everything: our creation, talents, health, success in undertakings, redemption, call to the Christian life or to the priesthood, and so forth.

To proclaim the greatness, magnificence, and fidelity of God is the duty of the priest. Even more, it is his honor and joy to give this witness. God is greater than we could ever think or imagine. To him we owe the debt of adoration, praise, thanksgiving, love, and propitiation or reparation, as Jesus has taught us. From him we request all we need for body and soul. To him we should be faithful in every little detail in our lives.

That is what religion is all about. It is the recognition of God with the mind, the heart, and our actions. His will, his eternal law, also written into the human conscience when conscience has not been deformed, should guide all of our actions. In this sense, religion is not optional. It is obligatory. It would be dishonest if we were to refuse to recognize our Creator and the Divine Providence that keeps all things in the proper order. A human being who dared to deny God this practical recognition should be considered foolish. The Second Vatican Council testifies: "Without the Creator the creature would disappear. . . . When God is forgotten . . . the creature itself grows unintelligible."[5]

The priest, as prophet of the transcendent God, exposes secularism as unacceptable. To live and act as if God did not exist is a mistaken, poorly formulated ideology that does not hold up under examination and is harmful in private and public life. It is one of the challenges of our time that the priest cannot ignore. As the Holy Father, Pope Benedict XVI, said to the plenary assembly of the Pontifical Council for Culture on March 8, 2008, "Secularization, which presents itself in cultures by imposing a world and humanity without reference to Transcendence, is invading every aspect of daily life and developing a mentality in which God is effectively absent, wholly or partially, from human life and awareness."

The entire life of the priest, apostle of the transcendent God, should be a way of shouting to people: "Lift up your hearts!" If the people can sincerely reply: "We have lifted them up to the Lord", then the priest has succeeded. It is the priest who preaches that God is Providence, that the invisible hand of God is never absent from human history, with all its vicissitudes, earthquakes, tsunami, pestilence, and hurricanes. It is the priest who finds in the Christian faith the reassuring word to say to the terminally ill person, to the soldier or athlete who is having one foot amputated, to the young widow who has lost her husband in an airplane accident and has four children, to the orphans whose father has been shot dead by thieves, to the mother whose only

[5] *Gaudium et Spes* (December 7, 1965), 36.

son who just graduated as a medical doctor has been killed by security agents who mistook him for a wanted terrorist, and also to a people suffering largely because of the errors of an inefficient government. It is the ministry of the priest to help all such people realize that God has not abandoned or forgotten them. In order to carry out this delicate and difficult ministry, the priest needs to be in solidarity with people who suffer, so that he shares with them his faith, trust, and hope in God. He should become "a minister of hope for others".[6]

6. The Priest, Prophet of the Meaning of Life on Earth

Many people on earth seem disoriented. They are not sure from where they come, why they exist on earth, where they are going, and how they can get there. They want to see meaning in their life on earth. If the priest does not explain to them the answers to these fundamental questions, who will do it for them?

The priest will be rendering them an important service if he makes it clear to them that God created them, that life on earth should be seen in terms of preparation for eternal life, and that only God can give to the human heart everlasting happiness in the beatific vision. Life on earth is not one monotonous activity after another. It is not a heap of scattered mosaics without unity, meaning, or design. The dock worker, the factory laborer, the garbage collector, the doorkeeper in a large establishment, the cook who has to repeat the same operation every day for years, the taxi driver who is going nowhere and everywhere and who often has

[6] Benedict XVI, *Spe Salvi* (November 30, 2007), 34.

to bring clients to the same destination, and even the specialized surgeon who each day repeats the same delicate operation—all of these people need to see a clear meaning in their lives and in the details of their daily work, which are often like those of the day before.

Those Christians are mistaken who think that religion consists in "saving their souls" in the sense of simply frequenting the sacraments and saying their daily prayers while they pay very little or no attention to their duties toward their neighbor. They have to learn that to be a good father, mother, spouse, son, daughter, citizen, worker, or official is an essential part of what it means to be a good Christian. A dishonest or negligent worker is not a good Christian. An authentic Christian is a good citizen. The Second Vatican Council uses rather strong language: "The Christian who neglects his temporal duties, neglects his duties toward his neighbor and even God, and jeopardizes his eternal salvation."[7]

The priest, as prophet of the meaning of our earthly life, should always help his people to see clearly that an authentic practice of Christianity relates life on earth to life in the world to come. *Gaudium et Spes* comes once more to our help: "While we are warned that it profits a man nothing if he gain the whole world and lose himself, the expectation of a new earth must not weaken but rather stimulate our concern for cultivating this one. For here grows the body of a new human family, a body which even now is able to give some kind of foreshadowing of the new age."[8]

Our Catholic faith gives joy to our life on earth. It gives our life a meaning and a sense of direction. It helps us to avoid the feeling of monotony in our daily work. It shows us

[7] *Gaudium et Spes*, 43.
[8] Ibid., 39.

how the universal call to holiness should be concretely lived according to each person's vocation and mission.[9] There are, therefore, canonized saints from all categories and vocations: spouses, parents, young people, adults, people from various professions in the world, clerics, and consecrated persons. The priest is the announcer, the indicator, the prophet of this life of hope, this clarity of vision, this psychological unity, this limpidity of action, and this sincere joy.

7. The Priest, Reflection of the Glory of the Transcendent God

When Moses came down from Mount Sinai, the skin of his face was shining, because he had conversed with God (cf. Ex 34:29–35; 2 Cor 3:7–18). This caused holy fear in the people.

The apparition of an angel caused fear and admiration in Manoah and his wife (cf. Judg 13:6–20) and in Zechariah (cf. Lk 1:12).

The members of the Sanhedrin saw the face of Saint Stephen shining when the saint contemplated the glory of God (cf. Acts 6:15; 7:55–56).

Yet more splendent was the transfiguration of Jesus in the presence of three of his Apostles (cf. Mt 17:2; Lk 9:29).

Our prayer is that the priest may be so united with God in prayer and in the contemplation of divine realities that people who interact with him become struck by a reflection of the divine. It would be beautiful if they came away from him with the conviction that they had been with a man of God.

---

[9] Cf. Vatican Council II, *Lumen Gentium* (November 21, 1964), 40–41.

8. *The Sacred Liturgy Helps Us*

The sacred liturgy often calls our attention to the transcendent glory and majesty of God. It uses expressions such as the following: almighty and eternal God; most merciful Father; God of mercy and of all consolation; we supplicate and beg you; accept with benevolence, O Lord; deign to accept in our favor; we offer to your divine majesty from the gifts that you have given us; look on our offerings in a serene and benign way; may he [Jesus] make us an everlasting gift pleasing to you; and so forth. Like a summary of this spirit of adoration before the divine majesty, the Prayer over the Gifts for Tuesday of the First Week of Advent runs thus: "Lord, we are nothing without you. As you sustain us with your mercy, receive our prayers and offerings."[10]

This attitude of profound respect before the divine transcendence is necessary especially in today's world, with its many distractions and the temptation to pride and irreverence. We go on our knees before God, "who alone has immortality and dwells in unapproachable light, whom no man has ever seen or can see. To him be honor and eternal dominion. Amen" (1 Tim 6:16).

---

[10] *Roman Missal.*

III

THE SINNER INVITED TO REPENTANCE

1. Sin Is an Offense against God

The meeting with Jesus and the continuous effort to follow him become damaged or even completely ruined by sin. Sin is an offense against God. It is an action against God's love for us. It estranges our hearts from the love of God. Saint Augustine describes sin as "love of self even to contempt of God".[1] The *Catechism of the Catholic Church* defines it thus: "Sin is an offense against reason, truth, and right conscience; it is failure in genuine love for God and neighbor caused by a perverse attachment to certain goods. . . . It has been defined as 'an utterance, a deed, or a desire contrary to the eternal law'."[2]

Sin is in the first place an offense against God, a rejection of God by man. God tells us through the prophet Jeremiah: "My people have committed two evils: they have forsaken me, the fountain of living waters, and hewed out cisterns for themselves, broken cisterns, that can hold no water" (Jer 2:13). Isaiah the prophet had himself earlier also accused the people of abandoning the Lord: "Hear, O heavens, and give ear, O earth; for the LORD has spoken: 'Sons have I reared and brought up, but they have rebelled against me. The ox knows its owner, and the donkey its master's crib; but Israel

---

[1] *De civitate Dei* 14.28.
[2] CCC 1849.

does not know, my people does not understand.' . . . They have forsaken the LORD, they have despised the Holy One of Israel, they are utterly estranged" (Is 1:2–4).

2. The Consciousness of Sin

It is important that the priest have, as far as it is possible for us, a clear idea of the holiness of God and of the evil of sin. There is a lamentable lessening of the consciousness of sin in the modern world. Far too many people are not clear on, or are not convinced of, the objective evil of some human acts. There are even some who hold to the theory that many people are practically incapable of committing a mortal sin. I would imagine that such a person might change his theory if his nice car were stolen. Those who hold such abstruse theories should tell us what to make of acts of terrorism; the killing of innocent persons; abortion; infanticide; euthanasia; adultery; the well-organized attack against marriage and the family; bank robbery; corruption in public life, which brings so much suffering to so many people; hatred of the Church, of religion, and even of God; the persecution of people because of their religious convictions; and finally, the violation of vows by some priests or consecrated people. If anyone still wants a catalogue of grave sins, let him read what Saint Paul writes to the Galatians (5:19–21), or to the Romans (1:28–32), or to the Corinthians (1 Cor 6:9–10), or to the Ephesians (5:3–5), or to the Colossians (3:5–8), or otherwise to Timothy (1 Tim 1:9–10, 2 Tim 3:2–5).

There is no doubt that sin is a very grave evil, denounced many times by Holy Scripture. To have some idea of the evil that sin does, it is enough to look at the Cross. The Son of God, the Innocent One, suffers atrocious pains because of our sins. The prophet Isaiah does not remain silent:

> He was despised and rejected by men;
>> a man of sorrows, and acquainted with grief. . . .
> Surely he has borne our griefs
>> and carried our sorrows;
> yet we esteemed him stricken,
>> struck down by God, and afflicted.
> But he was wounded for our transgressions,
>> he was bruised for our iniquities. . . .
> When he makes himself an offering for sin,
>> he shall see his offspring, he shall prolong his days.
>
> (Is 53:3, 4, 5, 10)

Every sinner should reflect on what sin has done to Jesus our Savior.

3. Accepting One's Fault

If the sinner wants to be liberated, the first condition is that one accepts one's fault. The Church teaches us in the penitential act at the beginning of the Eucharistic celebration to repent, to accept our fault, and to confess that we are sinners. She teaches us to say: "through my fault, through my fault, through my most grievous fault". Some people are tempted to say the contrary: "through the fault of my family member, through the fault of my colleagues, and through the most grievous fault of my superiors". A person cannot be on the road to healing until the person accepts fault where fault exists.

To the person who enters a crisis because he disobeys—possibly a religious or a priest—the *Imitation of Christ* gives unambiguous advice: "Run here or there, you will find no rest, but in an humble subjection under the government of a superior. The imagination and changing of places have deceived many."[3] It further advises: "Occasions do not make a man frail, but show what he is."[4]

If a priest declares: "I have a crisis with my bishop", how can we reply? Perhaps it is true. But it could be that he has a crisis, not with his bishop, but with the kneeler in front of the Blessed Sacrament, where he has not been seen for some time. Or perhaps he has a crisis with the examination of conscience, with daily mental prayer, or with the Rosary, because for a week now he has declared himself so busy with parish meetings that there was no time left for prayer!

A person could become the architect of his own misery. He could construct for himself a psychological prison, put himself inside, install an iron gate, lock the gate, and put the key into his pocket. Then he could turn around and lament: "They have put me in prison." But one could answer him: "Who put you in prison? You have the key in your pocket. You will come out when, by the grace of God, you decide to come out. You are the architect and also the builder of your own misery. No one can take your serenity away from you without your permission." No doubt, the grace of God initiates, accompanies, and brings to a happy conclusion the conversion of the sinner. But God wants the cooperation of the sinner. God, who created us without our cooperation, will not justify us without our cooperation.[5]

The liberation of the sinner begins, by the grace of God, on the day on which the sinner accepts guilt, at the moment when he decides to make a "U-turn". Healing begins when

---

[3] Thomas à Kempis, *Imitation of Christ* 1.9.1.

[4] Ibid., 1.16.4.

[5] "Qui fecit te sine te, non te iustificabit sine te", St. Augustine, *Sermo 169*, 13.

the prodigal son comes to himself and says: "How many of my father's hired servants have bread enough and to spare, but I perish here with hunger! I will arise and go to my father, and I will say to him, 'Father, I have sinned against heaven and before you; I am no longer worthy to be called your son'" (Lk 15:17–19).

4. Liberation from Sin

The sacred liturgy often prays for liberation from our sins, for our conversion, and for God's forgiveness. In Baptism we are liberated from original sin and, in the case of adults, also from personal sins. The Lamb of God who takes away the sins of the world is invoked especially at Holy Mass. Again Isaiah speaks:

> By his knowledge shall the righteous one, my servant,
>   make many to be accounted righteous;
>   and he shall bear their iniquities.
> Therefore I will divide him a portion with the great,
>   and he shall divide the spoil with the strong;
> because he poured out his soul to death,
> and was numbered with the transgressors;
> yet he bore the sin of many,
>   and made intercession for the transgressors.
>
> (Is 53:11–12)

The Fourth Eucharistic Prayer notes that when man by disobedience lost the friendship of God, God did not abandon him to the power of death but, in his mercy, came to the help of all men so that those who seek him may find him. Repentance and pardon are themes prominent in the Lenten liturgy.

5. Sinners in the Church

The Church, as the Mystical Body of Christ, is one, holy, catholic, and apostolic. At the same time, not all members of the Church always live with fidelity their new life in Christ. Some are indeed sinners, as the history of the Church shows. But as the disobedience of Adam led to the condemnation of all, so, by the obedience of Jesus Christ, "the grace of God and the free gift in the grace of that one man Jesus Christ abounded for many" (Rom 5:15). Saint Paul contrasts the universality of sin and death with the universality of salvation in Christ: "As one man's trespass led to condemnation for all men, so one man's act of righteousness leads to acquittal and life for all men" (Rom 5:18).[6]

The priest should preach holiness and the call to everyone to be holy. The Second Vatican Council is clear: "Thus it is evident to everyone, that all the faithful of Christ of whatever rank or status, are called to the fullness of the Christian life and to the perfection of charity."[7] At the same time, the priest does not take away from sinners all hope. Jesus invites sinners to repent and to come to take a seat at the table of the Kingdom that he was inaugurating. To the scribes and Pharisees who decided to be scandalized because Jesus sat at table with many publicans and sinners, the response of our Lord was not long in coming: "Those who are well have no need of a physician, but those who are sick; I came not to call the righteous, but sinners" (Mk 2:17). Saint Paul did not hesitate to write to his disciple Timothy: "The saying is sure and worthy of full acceptance, that Christ Jesus came into the world to save sinners. And I am the foremost of sin-

[6] Cf. *CCC* 402.
[7] *Lumen Gentium* (November 21, 1964), 40.

ners; but I received mercy for this reason, that in me, as the foremost, Jesus Christ might display his perfect patience for an example to those who were to believe in him for eternal life" (1 Tim 1:15–16).[8]

The priest should follow his Master Jesus and go in search of the lost sheep (cf. Lk 15:1–7). He should invite sinners to conversion, without which there is no entry into the Kingdom. He should preach to them the consoling doctrine of the mercy of the Father and that "there will be more joy in heaven over one sinner who repents than over ninety-nine righteous persons who need no repentance" (Lk 15:7).[9] To his Church, Jesus gives the power and the ministry to forgive sins in his Name.

6. God Is Rich in Mercy

Holy Scripture and the sacred liturgy teach us that God is merciful. Saint Paul writes to the Ephesians: "God, who is rich in mercy, out of the great love with which he loved us, even when we were dead through our trespasses, made us alive together with Christ (by grace you have been saved)" (Eph 2:4–5). Therefore there is hope for the sinner who repents.

The sinner should listen to the voice of love and to the appeal from God. In the short Reading at Lauds this Monday, God tells us: "If you will obey my voice and keep my covenant, you shall be my own possession among all peoples; for all the earth is mine, and you shall be to me a kingdom of priests and a holy nation" (Ex 19:5–69).

[8] Cf. *CCC* 827.
[9] Cf. *CCC* 545.

At Midday Prayer today, the short Reading continues to reassure us:

> But you are merciful to all, for you can do all things,
> and you overlook men's sins, that they may repent.
> For you love all things that exist,
> and you loathe none of the things which you have made,
> for you would not have made anything if you had hated it.
>
> (Wis 11:23–24)

The short Reading at Lauds tomorrow will see the Lord again inviting us to conversion:

> "Return to me with all your heart,
> with fasting, with weeping, and with mourning;
> and tear your hearts and not your garments."
> Return to the LORD, your God,
> for he is gracious and merciful,
> slow to anger, and abounding in mercy,
> and repents of evil.
>
> (Joel 2:12–13)

In the opening prayer for the votive Mass of Divine Mercy, the Church prays the God of infinite mercy to increase the faith of his people, so that they may understand better with what love they have been created, with whose blood they have been redeemed, and with whose Spirit they have been renewed.

Let us conclude by begging the Lord with the Church as in the Collect of the Mass of today: "God our savior, bring us back to you and fill our minds with your wisdom. May we be enriched by our observance of Lent. Grant this through Christ our Lord. Amen."

IV

PENANCE

We shall reflect on penance as virtue, and then as a sacrament.

1. The Necessity of the Virtue of Penance

Jesus, innocent and without sin, had no need of penance. And yet he fasted for forty days and forty nights.

We, on the contrary, have need of penance because we have inherited original sin and have also committed personal sins and have weaknesses. Jesus, as the prophets had done earlier, called for conversion and penance; first of all to conversion of heart, to interior penance, and only later to exterior works of penance, "sackcloth and ashes". "Interior repentance is a radical reorientation of our whole life, a return, a conversion to God with all our heart, an end of sin, a turning away from evil, with repugnance toward the evil actions we have committed. At the same time it entails the desire and resolution to change one's life, with hope in God's mercy and trust in the help of his grace."[1]

Conversion of heart and interior penance are expressed in external gestures that are traditionally grouped under three

[1] *CCC* 1431.

headings: fasting, prayer, and almsgiving. They express conversion with reference to oneself, to God, and to one's neighbor. The different forms of mortification fall under these three titles.

Our beloved Lord insists on the necessity of penance. He began preaching by the call: "Repent, for the kingdom of heaven is at hand" (Mt 4:17). "The kingdom of heaven has suffered violence, and men of violence take it by force" (Mt 11:12). "Unless you repent you will all likewise perish" (Lk 13:5).

Saint Paul has no doubts: "I do not run aimlessly, I do not box as one beating the air; but I pommel my body and subdue it, lest after preaching to others I myself should be disqualified" (1 Cor 9:26–27). And in his Letter to the Corinthians, he goes into great detail about what he has had to suffer in the preaching of the Gospel (cf. 2 Cor 11:16–33).

Chapter 12 of the second book of the *Imitation of Christ* speaks of the royal way of the Holy Cross. Its advice merits careful meditation. Among other things, it admonishes us:

> Know for certain that you must lead a dying life, and the more a man dies to himself the more he begins to live to God. No man is fit to comprehend heavenly things who has not resigned himself to suffer adversities for Christ. Nothing is more acceptable to God, nothing more wholesome for you in this world, than to suffer willingly for Christ. . . . If, indeed, there had been anything better and more beneficial to man's salvation than suffering, Christ certainly would have showed it by word and example. For he manfully exhorts both his disciples that followed him and all that desire to follow him to bear the cross, saying: "If any one will come after me, let him deny himself and take up his cross and follow me." So that when we have read and searched all let this be the final conclusion, that "through many tribulations we must enter into the kingdom of God".

2. The "Christological" Basis for Mortification

Jesus had no need of penance or mortification for himself, because he was innocent. And he had no weaknesses like us. He had nothing of which to repent because he was without sin.

Nevertheless, Jesus "mortified" himself considerably. Born in a stable at Bethlehem, he had to take refuge in Egypt to avoid the cruelty of Herod. In his public ministry, he trekked much and had "nowhere to lay his head" (Mt 8:20). Falsely accused, unjustly condemned, abandoned by all his Apostles save one, he suffered an atrocious crucifixion and had to receive a donated tomb from Joseph of Arimathea. Jesus suffered all of this "for love of us and for our salvation".[2]

The priest, *alter Christus*, has to learn from his Master. The priest, no doubt, will do mortification because he has need of it personally to demonstrate his own repentance, to discipline his character, to strengthen his will, and to become better grounded in virtue, and in this way to carry out his mission with greater efficacy. All of this is true. But there is more. The priest should seek to contribute to the salvation of his people under Christ, with Christ, through Christ, and in Christ. His love of God, his pain at seeing the love of God offended by people, his consequent desire to make reparation—all this urges him to embrace and undertake acts of mortification.

3. The Sacred Liturgy Insists on Penance

In the liturgical year, Lent as preparation for Easter, and Good Friday in memory of the death of our Savior are

[2] Credo.

special times of penance. These are ideal times for spiritual exercises, penitential liturgies, pilgrimages, and voluntary mortifications such as fasting, almsgiving, and acts of solidarity with the needy.[3]

The liturgy sees penance as a way to spiritual renewal. In the Collect of the Mass of Wednesday this week[4] the Church begs God our Father to look on the people consecrated to him and to grant that, mortifying their bodies by abstinence, they may be renewed in spirit and produce the fruit of good works. On Friday the Collect returns to the same theme and prays that the communal exercise of bodily mortification may bring to all of us true spiritual renewal.[5]

4. Forms of Penance

The most fundamental forms of mortification, which also have less risk of self-illusion, are those mortifications that are part and parcel of our vocation and mission and have not been specifically chosen by us. Here are some examples: to accept heat or cold without complaining; to be gracious toward our co-workers, especially those whom we may not like much; to receive visitors when we are rather tired or busy; and to deal with difficult people. For some bishops, it might be mortifying to put on liturgical vestments and the mitre in a hot and humid climate, to answer letters that

[3] Cf. Vatican Council II, *Sacrosanctum Concilium* (December 4, 1963), 109–10; *Code of Canon Law*, can. 1249–53; *CCC* 1434–39.

[4] "Lord, look upon us and hear our prayer. By the good works you inspire, help us to discipline our bodies and to be renewed in spirit. Grant this through our Lord Jesus Christ, your Son, who lives and reigns with you and the Holy Spirit, one God, for ever and ever."

[5] "Lord, may our observance of Lent help to renew us and prepare us to celebrate the death and resurrection of Christ, who lives and reigns with you and the Holy Spirit, one God, for ever and ever."

seem never to end, or to prepare five-yearly reports for the Roman Curia! For a person who works in the Roman Curia, it could be mortifying to have to work far away from the usual diocesan or parish situation, to prepare the draft of a document that gets radically modified by the assembly or by the superior, to receive no public applause for an excellent document on which one has worked day and night, to have to participate in one meeting after another, to study documents that are rather long, and to have to sacrifice one's opinion because the other members of the commission have a different view. Someone could also be mortified because he did not receive even a word of thanks for a job well done, or because he feels forgotten once again, maybe in truth, or perhaps because only he thinks so. It can also become difficult for some official to resist the temptation to engage in ecclesiastical politics or to look for someone who can put in a word so that he can receive the appointment he desires!

As can be seen, there is no lack of occasions to mortify ourselves in the carrying out of our daily work. And then there are mortifications that we freely choose: prayer, fasting, the sacrifice of some drink or rest. Discretion is needed in order not to fall into extremes, or into self-deceit or self-canonization. Sometimes the spiritual director can advise.

In the short Reading at Vespers this evening, Saint Paul speaks to us: "I appeal to you therefore, brethren, by the mercies of God, to present your bodies as a living sacrifice, holy and acceptable to God, which is your spiritual worship" (Rom 12:1).

If a follower of Christ has the spirit of penance, he could express this spirit in works of freely chosen mortification. In this sense we could say that such acts of mortification dispose us and help us to accept the mortifications that are imposed on us as part of our vocation and mission, and to do so with due serenity and a sense of faith.

5. The Sacrament of Penance

Sin is in the first place an offense against God and a damage of communion with him. In the case of a mortal sin, there is a total break of communion with God. But at the same time, sin damages communion with the Church. Therefore conversion is not only for pardon from God but also for reconciliation with the Church. All of this is expressed liturgically in the rite of the sacrament of Penance, or Reconciliation. The celebration of this sacrament has been developed by the Church over the centuries under the guidance of the Holy Spirit.

There is no doubt that Jesus gave to his Apostles the power and ministry to liberate people from sin in his Name: "Receive the Holy Spirit. If you forgive the sins of any, they are forgiven; if you retain the sins of any, they are retained" (Jn 20:22–23). "In imparting to his apostles his own power to forgive sins the Lord also gives them the authority to reconcile sinners with the Church. This ecclesial dimension of their task is expressed most notably in Christ's solemn words to Simon Peter: 'I will give you the keys of the kingdom of heaven, and whatever you bind on earth shall be bound in heaven, and whatever you loose on earth shall be loosed in heaven' (Mt 16:19)."[6]

6. The Administration of the Sacrament of Penance

The administration of the Sacrament of Penance is one of the most demanding acts of the priest's ministry. It demands time, concentration, patience, theological knowledge, and

[6] CCC 1444.

pastoral experience and love. If the priest is not armed with strong convictions founded on faith and on great zeal, he could be tempted to postpone or to rush quickly the ministry of the confessional. Or he may administer the sacrament in such a way that the penitents draw the conclusion that the priest prefers that they did not come. It would be helpful for the priest to consider the fact that, for most of the lay faithful, the confessional is practically the only opportunity that they have to receive spiritual attention and direction from the priest on a one-to-one basis. It is not for nothing that the Curé d'Ars, Saint John Mary Vianney, is the patron of parish priests. He sat in the confessional for seventeen hours a day. He snatched so many souls from the devil that the devil one day burned his bed. Providentially, our saint was not in the room at that time!

Each of us can put some questions to himself in an examination of conscience on a matter of such great importance. How deep and strong is my faith in the sacrament of Penance? What is the name of my regular confessor? With what regular frequency do I confess to him? If I am a diocesan bishop, how much attention do I give to discussion of the pastoral ministry of this sacrament in my meetings with my priests?

We all know the resounding impact when the Holy Father sits in the confessional in Saint Peter's Basilica even for half an hour or an hour. The message and teaching are clear and strong. Of course, the diocesan bishop cannot hear confessions often, like his parish priests. But who does not appreciate the encouragement that the bishop gives to his priests and to the people of his diocese when he sits in the confessional for some time during Lent and Advent? A Roman Curia bishop or priest can ask himself questions on the matter.

From time to time, one hears of some priest who has dared to impart collective absolution without taking into consideration the stringent conditions laid down by the *Code of Canon Law*, canons 960–63, or by the motu proprio *Misericordia Dei*, issued by the Servant of God Pope John Paul II on April 7, 2002. The diocesan bishop will seek to help such a priest appreciate the reasons for the directives of Holy Mother Church and to follow them.

7. *Confession and the Amendment of Our Lives*

In our regular confessions, there is the risk that we could be confessing the same venial sins or weaknesses without visible signs of amendment of our lives. The solution is not to stop confessing such sins. Rather, we should seek to go to the roots of such defects if possible, by identifying the dominant passions or weaknesses that seem to be the cause and perhaps concentrating our efforts of amendment on these. Without falling into scruples, we should trust in God. His grace could be working in us in ways that we may not know. We should continue as children who love God, their Father. We should not get discouraged. We should remain always in the certainty that God loves us. To him be honor and glory forever and ever.

V

THE FAITH OF THE
PRIEST IN JESUS CHRIST

"In many and various ways God spoke of old to our fathers by the prophets; but in these last days he has spoken to us by a Son, whom he appointed the heir of all things, through whom also he created the ages" (Heb 1:1–2). "And the Word became flesh and dwelt among us" (Jn 1:14).

Jesus Christ is at the center of history. The Incarnation of the Word of God, together with the work of salvation accomplished by him, is the most important event in all of human history, and indeed in the cosmos. Therefore, for the priest who wants to meet Jesus and follow him, faith in the Incarnate Word is of primary importance.

1. The Priest Believes in Jesus Christ

The priest knows that Jesus Christ is not just a prophet, a holy founder of a religion, a great preacher, and a miracle worker. He is much more. With Saint Peter, the priest confesses: "You are the Christ, the Son of the living God" (Mt 16:16). Jesus Christ is "the only Son of God, eternally begotten of the Father, God from God, Light from Light, true God from true God, begotten, not made, consubstantial [one in Being] with the Father".[1]

---

[1] Credo.

It is this only begotten Son of the Father who, remaining always God, in the fullness of time took on human nature. "By the power of the Holy Spirit he was born of the Virgin Mary, and became man", "for us men and for our salvation".[2] He and the Father are one (cf. Jn 10:30). To Philip and the other Apostles, Jesus says: "He who has seen me has seen the Father. . . . Believe me that I am in the Father and the Father is in me" (Jn 14:9, 11).

It is this Son of God who, taking on human nature, does the work of our salvation and, crucified and risen, remains with us in his Church, which celebrates the sacred mysteries of his passion, death, Resurrection, and Ascension. Behold Jesus Christ, who is the center of our faith and who gives meaning to the priest in his life and his mission.

2. A Personal Relationship with Jesus

The entire life of the priest should be a continuous living with Christ and in Christ. "All that Jesus began to do and teach" (Acts 1:1) is, for the priest, guide and way. Jesus is for him "the way, and the truth, and the life" (Jn 14:6).

In a very special way, the priest is in contact with Christ in the Church and through the Church. "Christ is always present in His Church, especially in her liturgical celebrations. He is present in the sacrifice of the Mass, not only in the person of His minister, 'the same [one] now offering, through the ministry of priests, who formerly offered himself on the cross', but especially under the Eucharistic species."[3] All of this demands much faith, devotion, and fidelity from the priest in the celebration of Holy Mass and in the veneration of the Eucharistic Jesus outside the Mass.

---

[2] Ibid.

[3] Vatican Council II, *Sacrosanctum Concilium* (December 4, 1963), 7.

It is helpful to the faith of the priest to reflect that in the Eucharistic celebration, his union with Christ as his minister, his sacramental instrument, is so close that at consecration the priest says: "This is my Body." If he were to say: "This is the Body of Christ", transubstantiation would not take place.

Moreover, the Council continues, Christ "is present in the sacraments, so that when a man baptizes it is really Christ Himself who baptizes". What an honor for the priest who administers the sacraments. What an appeal to him to unite himself closely with Christ the supreme and eternal High Priest.

The rest of the sacred liturgy continues to invite the priest to live his union with Christ, who "is present in His word, since it is He Himself who speaks when the holy scriptures are read in the Church. He is present, lastly, when the Church prays and sings, for He promised: 'Where two or three are gathered together in my name, there am I in the midst of them.' "[4]

The faith of the priest will urge him to remain for long hours before the Most Blessed Sacrament of the Altar, to put before Jesus his projects, to ask for light and blessing on his initiatives in the apostolate, and to give thanks for graces received. It is especially in prayer, liturgical and personal, that the faith of the priest in Christ manifests itself and grows.

3. The Priest Follows the Obedient Jesus

The priest has as Master the one who said: "My food is to do the will of him who sent me, and to accomplish his work" (Jn 4:34). At Gethsemane, Jesus prayed thus: "Father, if you

[4] Ibid.

are willing, remove this chalice from me; nevertheless not my will, but yours, be done" (Lk 22:42).

If the priest absorbs and lives this example of his Master, many of his problems in the areas of obedience and harmony or unity in the apostolate would find a solution in faith and love. His whole life would be like an offertory procession, full of interior peace and self-sacrifice.

4. The Priest Follows the Zealous Jesus

Jesus was 100 percent occupied with the things of his Father. Even at the tender age of twelve, he knew how to give priority to the demands of attention to his eternal Father before considering the pain of Mary and Joseph, whom he no doubt loved very much. When they found him in the temple on the third day, after a painful search, he asked them: "How is it that you sought me? Did you not know that I must be in my Father's house?" (Lk 2:49).

At the beginning of his public life, when Jesus saw people trading in the temple, "making a whip of cords, he drove them all, with the sheep and oxen, out of the temple; and he poured out the coins of the money-changers and overturned their tables. And he told those who sold the pigeons, 'Take these things away; you shall not make my Father's house a house of trade'" (Jn 2:15–16). It is marvelous how Jesus single-handedly carried out this operation. And the evangelist informs us of how this demonstration of zeal struck the Apostles: "His disciples remembered that it was written, 'Zeal for your house will consume me'" (Jn 2:17).

Jesus was so taken up with the urgency of evangelization that at times there did not even remain time for meals! And the evangelist Mark adds: "And when his friends heard it, they went out to seize him, for they said, 'He is beside himself' " (Mk 3:21). Jesus was not beside himself. But he was no doubt full of zeal for the work of his Father.

The priest has his Model in front of him. The Second Vatican Council says that zeal for the promotion of liturgical pastoral action is a sign of the providential designs of God in our time.[5] In a more general way, the Council encourages priests in their ministry and urges them to be zealous: "Priests should remember that in performing their office, they are never alone, but strengthened by the power of Almighty God, and believing in Christ who called them to share in his Priesthood, they should devote themselves to their ministry with complete trust, knowing that God can cause charity to grow in them."[6]

5. Reverence for the Name of Jesus

The priest gives great respect to the Name of Jesus. The name of the Redeemer means salvation, hope given, and the love of God toward fallen humanity. As Saint Paul testifies, Christ Jesus, though he was in the form of God, emptied himself, taking the form of a servant. He humbled himself and became obedient unto death, even death on a cross. "Therefore God has highly exalted him and bestowed on him the name which is above every name, that at the name of Jesus every knee should bow, in heaven and on earth and under the earth, and every tongue confess that Jesus Christ is Lord, to the glory of God the Father" (Phil 2:9–11). It helps to imagine with what reverence and love the Virgin Mary

[5] Cf. ibid., 43.
[6] *Presbyterorum Ordinis* (December 7, 1965), 22.

and Saint Joseph must have pronounced the Holy Name of Jesus.

The Church celebrates on January 3 the memorial of the Most Holy Name of Jesus and prays the almighty Father, who has built the salvation of humanity on his Incarnate Word, mercifully to give his people the knowledge that there is no other Name to invoke apart from that of his only-begotten Son.

The Name of Jesus is the most famous Name since the beginning of the world. It is the Name most loved. This Name is a Person. It is life, salvation, plan for living, hope, and love. For the Name of Jesus the martyrs have laid down their lives and the confessors and virgins have consecrated their entire earthly existence. It is the Name that all of us want to have in our hearts and on our lips in our last moments in this valley of tears.

The priest will always seek to show reverence for the Most Holy Name of Jesus and to convince his people to do the same. In the Prayer after Communion the Church prays that our names also may be written in heaven.

6. Jesus Reassures Us

The faith of the priest in Jesus the Savior is reinforced by the many reassurances that Jesus gives us in the Gospels.

Many times he tells the Apostles not to be afraid (cf. Mt 8:26; 28:10; Mk 4:40; Lk 5:10; Jn 6:20; Acts 18:9; 27:24).

The night before he suffered, Jesus spoke to his Apostles in a particular way as a father to his beloved children whom he was about to leave behind on earth. "Let not your hearts be troubled; believe in God, believe also in me" (Jn 14:1). "I will ask the Father, and he will give you another

Counselor, to be with you for ever, even the Spirit of truth, whom the world cannot receive, because it neither sees him nor knows him" (Jn 14:16–17). "The Counselor, the Holy Spirit, whom the Father will send in my name, he will teach you all things, and bring to your remembrance all that I have said to you. Peace I leave with you; my peace I give to you; not as the world gives do I give to you. Let not your hearts be troubled, neither let them be afraid" (Jn 14:26–27).

The priest, therefore, should put his trust in Jesus, repose his hope in him, see clearly that the Church belongs to Jesus and not to the priest, and therefore remain in his life and in his mission very firm in his faith in Jesus Christ.

VI

JESUS, THE ONLY SAVIOR
AND THE CENTER OF PREACHING

1. Jesus Christ, the Only Savior

It is of crucial importance for the life and ministry of the priest, and therefore for the entire ministry of the Church, that the unicity and universality of the mystery of salvation in Jesus Christ be explained, appreciated, believed, and lived.

The New Testament speaks with clarity. "We have seen and testify that the Father has sent his Son as the Savior of the world" (1 Jn 4:14). "Behold, the Lamb of God, who takes away the sin of the world!" (Jn 1:29) is the testimony of John the Baptist. Peter proclaims before the Sanhedrin the solemn Christian faith: "There is salvation in no one else, for there is no other name under heaven given among men by which we must be saved" (Acts 4:12). In his speech in the house of Cornelius, Peter continues along the same lines, testifying to Jesus the Redeemer: "Jesus Christ (he is Lord of all) . . . judge of the living and the dead. . . . Every one who believes in him receives forgiveness of sins through his name" (Acts 10:36, 42, 43). The evangelist John is very clear: "For God so loved the world that he gave his only-begotten Son, that whoever believes in him should not perish but have eternal life. For God sent the Son into the world, not to condemn the world, but that the world might be saved through him. He who believes in him is not condemned; he who does not believe is condemned already, because he has not believed in the name of the only-begotten Son of God" (Jn 3:16–18). And Saint Paul speaks of the uniqueness of the mediatorship of Jesus Christ: God "desires all men to be saved and to come to the knowledge of the truth. For there is one God, and there is one mediator between God and men, the man Christ Jesus, who gave himself as a ransom for all" (1 Tim 2:4–6).

The faith of the Church is therefore that Jesus Christ is the one and only Savior for all and that there is no other savior. "The Church firmly believes that Christ, who died and was raised up for all, can through His Spirit offer man the light and the strength to measure up to his supreme destiny. Nor has any other name under the heaven been given to man by which it is fitting for him to be saved."[1]

2. Definitive Revelation in Jesus Christ

It is therefore the duty and honor of the priest to preach that the New Covenant in Jesus Christ is complete and definitive. The Second Vatican Council teaches that Jesus Christ "perfected revelation by fulfilling it through his whole work of making Himself present and manifesting Himself: through His words and deeds, His signs and wonders, but especially though His death and glorious resurrection from the dead and final sending of the Spirit of truth. . . . The Christian dispensation, therefore, as the new and definitive covenant, will never pass away and we now await no further new pub-

[1] Vatican Council II, *Gaudium et Spes* (December 7, 1965), 10; cf. Congregation for the Doctrine of the Faith, *Dominus Jesus* (August 6, 2000), 13.

lic revelation before the glorious manifestation of our Lord Jesus Christ."[2]

In dialogue and collaboration with people of other religions, as well as in cultural dialogue, Christians should never forget this truth or try to put it in parentheses. We should exercise charity in truth. The truth about Christ does not threaten anyone. And Jesus himself has told us: "You will know the truth, and the truth will make you free" (Jn 8:32). Religion is proposed. It is not imposed. But dialogue is not promoted by doing damage to our Christian identity or destroying it altogether. Persons of other religions who respect us do not want to damage or destroy our Christian identity as a condition for dialogue. Indeed, if they succeeded in destroying it, there would be nobody left with whom they could dialogue!

As the Servant of God Pope John Paul II teaches in the great encyclical letter *Redemptoris Missio*,

> In the Gospel of St. John, this salvific universality of Christ embraces all the aspects of his mission of grace, truth and revelation: the Word is "the true light that enlightens every man" (Jn 1:9). And again, "no one has ever seen God; the only Son, who is in the bosom of the Father, he has made him known" (Jn 1:18; cf. Mt 11:27). God's revelation becomes definitive and complete through his only-begotten Son: "In many and various ways God spoke of old to our fathers by the prophets; but in these last days he has spoken to us by a Son, whom he appointed the heir of all things, through whom he also created the world" (Heb 1:1−2; cf. Jn 14:6).[3]

---

[2] *Dei Verbum* (November 18, 1965), 4; cf. Congregation for the Doctrine of the Faith, *Dominus Jesus*, 12.

[3] *Redemptoris Missio* (December 7, 1990), 5.

The Holy Father concludes:

> No one, therefore, can enter into communion with God except through Christ, by the working of the Holy Spirit. Christ's one, universal mediation, far from being an obstacle on the journey toward God, is the way established by God himself, a fact of which Christ is fully aware. Although participated forms of mediation of different kinds and degrees are not excluded, they acquire meaning and value *only* from Christ's own mediation, and they cannot be understood as parallel or complementary to his.[4]

This is the truth that saves us. It is necessary to hold firmly to, and to live, the oft-quoted words of our Redeemer: "I am the way, and the truth, and the life; no one comes to the Father, but by me" (Jn 14:6). The way in which the priest speaks with Jesus and about him, the way in which he follows him, and the way in which he makes him present to people and among people would be very different if Jesus were just one saving figure alongside others. The fact that Jesus is the one Savior for all explains the radicalism of discipleship and also why the priest is ready to make many sacrifices for the sake of Christ.

3. Jesus Christ, the Center of Preaching and Catechesis

It follows as a consequence that at the center of the preaching of the Church we find Jesus Christ in his mysteries. The Church preaches Christ crucified and risen. Pope John Paul II teaches: "At the heart of catechesis we find, in essence, a Person, the Person of Jesus of Nazareth, 'the only

[4] Ibid.

Son from the Father . . . full of grace and truth,' who suffered and died for us and who now, after rising, is living with us forever. It is Jesus who is 'the way, and the truth, and the life,' and Christian living consists in following Christ, the *sequela Christi*."[5] Pope Paul VI had insisted on the same centrality of Christ in evangelization in his postsynodal exhortation *Evangelii Nuntiandi* in 1975. He spoke specifically of the necessity of explicit proclamation of Jesus Christ: "The Good News proclaimed by the witness of life sooner or later has to be proclaimed by the word of life. There is no true evangelization if the name, the teaching, the life, the promises, the kingdom and the mystery of Jesus of Nazareth, the Son of God, are not proclaimed."[6]

The temptation for the one who preaches or who catechizes is to transmit his own opinions or the theses of some scholar, or to engage in theological acrobatics. Such a temptation is to be resisted. Pope John Paul II insists on the centrality of Christ: "Christocentricity in catechesis also means the intention to transmit not one's own teaching or that of some other master, but the teaching of Jesus Christ, the Truth that He communicates or, to put it more precisely, the Truth that He is. We must therefore say that in catechesis it is Christ, the Incarnate Word and Son of God, who is taught—everything else is taught with reference to Him—and it is Christ alone who teaches—anyone else teaches to the extent that he is Christ's spokesman, enabling Christ to teach with his lips."[7]

---

[5] *Catechesi Tradendae* (October 16, 1979), 5.
[6] *Evangelii Nuntiandi* (December 8, 1975), 22.
[7] *Catechesi Tradendae*, 6.

4. Jesus Christ, the Center of Liturgical Celebrations

It follows that in the sacred liturgy it is Christ in his mysteries that is celebrated. The Eucharistic celebration, in particular, is the memorial of Christ's paschal mystery celebrated sacramentally. The priest and the people do not come together to celebrate and admire one another. They have been convoked by the Holy Spirit to celebrate in a sacramental way the passion, death, and Resurrection of Jesus. In particular, the priest, the minister of Christ, should make every effort to carry out the sacred rites with the proper *ars celebrandi*, so that Christ is at the center of the attention of all. A mirror is dirty when it attracts attention to itself. It is clean when it permits the image of what should be seen to be clearly seen. The priest should ask himself whether a person seeing the way he celebrates Holy Mass and the way he preaches could apply to him the words of Jesus: "Let your light so shine before men, that they may see your good works and give glory to your Father who is in heaven" (Mt 5:16). The altar *versus populum* demands much discipline from the priest. He should resist the temptation to "stage a show" or to become "Reverend Showman".

One can also pose some questions regarding the construction of some churches called "modern". Do they really orient the mind toward God? Sacred art is helpful in this respect and should uplift us to celebrate the transcendent God or the Lord Jesus in his mysteries. When we think of some modern buildings that pass for churches, it would seem that some of them are rather celebrating the architect! They are horizontal rather than vertical in their message. They are often without that beauty and that sacredness of form which help to raise the mind to God. Some look like theaters or conference halls

or airport hangars. Certainly, not all churches can attain the
splendor and verticality of Saint Peter's Basilica in Vatican
City, or of the cathedrals of Milan, Cologne, Chartres, or
New York, or of the basilicas of the Immaculate Conception
in Washington, D.C., or of Notre Dame de la Paix in Yamoussoukro.[8] But even the cathedrals, parish churches, and
station chapels in regions of recent evangelization can, and
should, all transmit the message that God is transcendent. A
bell tower helps.

Moreover, inside the church building, prominence should
be given, not only to the altar, but also to the crucifix and
the tabernacle. Thank you, Holy Father,[9] because without
many words but with actions you show us that the crucifix
should occupy a central place in the Eucharistic celebration,
possibly on the altar. In some churches in the last forty years,
a fashion is developing to locate the tabernacle in a corner
or even in a pillar or a wall. This is mistaken. This was
never approved by the *Roman Missal*. In many churches the
tabernacle can very well occupy the central place behind the
altar. In any case, its position should be prominent, distin-
guished, and noble. Otherwise, people could enter a church
and begin to ask: "Where is the tabernacle?" Mary Mag-
dalen already lamented: "They have taken away my Lord,
and I do not know where they have laid him" (Jn 20:13).

Jesus in his mysteries should be at the center of our liturgical celebrations. The diocesan bishop and his diocesan commission for sacred art have the duty and also the right to
choose architects who share our faith, to dialogue with them,
and indeed to give them liturgical and theological indications. Gratitude is due to the Pontifical Commission for the

---

[8] Yamoussoukro is the capital of the Ivory Coast.
[9] Benedict XVI.

Cultural Goods of the Church for the orientation that it gives in this matter, in collaboration with the Congregation for Divine Worship and the Discipline of the Sacraments.

The Holy Father, in his Christmas speech to the Roman Curia on December 22, 2008, illustrates how at the center of celebrations at World Youth Day in Sydney in July 2008 was Jesus Christ, not the Pope. Pope Benedict said that World Youth Day pointed

> to the One who gathers us together, to that God who loves us all the way to the Cross. Thus, the Pope himself is not the star around which everything revolves. He is completely and solely a Vicar. He points beyond himself to the Other who is in our midst. In the end, the solemn liturgy is the centre of the whole event, because in it there takes place something that we ourselves cannot bring about, yet something for which we are always awaiting. Christ is present.[10]

The priest, therefore, should fix his attention on Jesus Christ, the one and only Savior and the center of the preaching and liturgy of the Church, and indeed of the entire Christian life.

---

[10] Speech, December 22, 2008, *L'Osservatore Romano*, weekly English edition, January 7, 2009, p. 12.

VII

THE PRIEST MEETS
JESUS IN HOLY SCRIPTURE

The priest appreciates very much the encounter he has with Jesus in Holy Scripture.

No doubt, the Word of God in Person is the only-begotten Son of God, born of the Father before all ages, Word of the Father made flesh (cf. Jn 1:14). But the divine Word has revealed himself during the course of the history of salvation and is witnessed to in the writings of the Old and New Testaments. Holy Scripture therefore contains the Word of God in a singular way.[1]

1. Sacred Scripture Is a Precious Heritage

Sacred Scripture is a most precious heritage of the Church. *Dei Verbum* teaches us that everything asserted by the inspired authors or sacred writers must be held to be asserted by the Holy Spirit. The books of Scripture teach firmly, faithfully, and without error those truths that God wanted put into the sacred writings for the sake of our salvation. Therefore "all Scripture is inspired by God and profitable for teaching, for reproof, for correction, and for training

[1] Cf. 2008 Synod of Bishops, prop. 3.

in righteousness, that the man of God may be complete, equipped for every good work" (2 Tim 3:16–17).[2]

The priest cannot fail to notice the high esteem in which the Second Vatican Council holds Holy Scripture. The Council in fact asserts: "The Church has always venerated the divine Scriptures just as she venerates the body of the Lord, since, especially in the sacred liturgy, she unceasingly receives and offers to the faithful the bread of life from the table both of God's word and of Christ's body."[3]

The priest who wants to meet Jesus has to take in hand the Sacred Book. In Sacred Scripture, Jesus speaks to us today. The Synod of Bishops in October 2008 therefore

> re-proposes with energy to all the faithful the encounter with Jesus, the Word of God made flesh, as an event of grace in the reading and the listening to the Sacred Scriptures. It remembers Saint Cyprian who gathers a thought shared with the Fathers: "Pay attention with diligence to prayer and to *Lectio divina*. When you pray you talk with God; when you read it is God who speaks with you" (*Ad Donatum*, 15).[4]

The Synod therefore had great hopes that from that assembly would flourish a new season of great love for Sacred Scripture on the part of the members of the Church, so that from their prayerful and faithful reading a deepening of relationship with the very Person of Jesus will gradually take place. The Synod desires that, as far as possible, every member of the faithful personally possess a copy of the Bible. The priest should be in the front line of the promotion of this devotion to the Bible.

[2] Cf. Vatican Council II, *Dei Verbum* (November 18, 1965), 11.

[3] Ibid., 21.

[4] 2008 Synod of Bishops, prop. 9.

2. Scripture and Liturgy

The sacred liturgy is the privileged place in which the Word of God expresses itself fully, in the celebration of the sacraments—especially of the Holy Eucharist—in the Liturgy of the Hours, and in the liturgical year. The mystery of salvation narrated in Holy Scripture finds in the liturgy its proper place to be proclaimed, to be heard, and to be put into action.[5]

Liturgical texts and symbols are, in great part, based on Holy Scripture. Just think, for example, on the Psalms and on the books of the Old and New Testaments read in the liturgy. "When the Sacred Scriptures are read in Church, it is God who speaks to his people, and Christ, present in his word itself, proclaims the Gospel."[6] Many prayers and antiphons are based on biblical images and concepts.

Numerous liturgical symbols and expressions could not be understood without their biblical references. Examples include paschal lamb, Lamb of God, Passover, offerings, Second Adam, Church, people of God, Lord God of hosts, propitiation, sacrifice, and intercession.

Ongoing study of Holy Scripture is therefore recommended to the minister of Christ.

3. Importance of Knowledge of the Bible

The Fathers of the Second Vatican Council insist that all clerics should hold fast to Holy Scripture through diligent

---

[5] Cf. ibid., prop. 14.
[6] General Instruction of the *Roman Missal*, 29.

spiritual reading and attentive and ongoing study. The Council recommends this in a special way to priests and to others, such as deacons and catechists, who are engaged in the ministry of the Word.[7] All of this applies in an eminent way to the bishop, who should be a model for other agents of evangelization.

They should maintain continued contact with the Scriptures, says the Council, "so that none of them will become 'an empty preacher of the word of God outwardly, who is not a listener to it inwardly'[8] since they must share the abundant wealth of the divine word with the faithful committed to them, especially in the sacred liturgy."[9] The Council recalls the famous saying of Saint Jerome: "For ignorance of the Scriptures is ignorance of Christ."[10]

4. The Priest, Lover of Holy Scripture

The priest should be a model of one who loves Holy Scripture. It is not absolutely necessary for him to have studied in the famous Biblical Institute in Rome before he can take the Bible in hand every day, preferably in front of Jesus in the Most Blessed Sacrament of the Altar. Before the Lord, and under the guidance of the Holy Spirit, the priest can read the sacred text each day for at least fifteen minutes. Such a devotion will not fail to enrich him with the surpassing knowledge of Christ Jesus (cf. Phil 3:8). It will inspire with divine fire his homilies and other writings. He will be better able to persuade his people to give more attention to

[7] Cf. *Dei Verbum*, 25.

[8] St. Augustine, *Sermo 179*, 1.

[9] *Dei Verbum*, 25.

[10] *Commentarium in Isaiam*, Prol., in *Patrologia latina*, ed. I.-P. Migne (Paris, 1844–1864), 24:17 (hereafter cited as PL).

Holy Scripture. Every priest or bishop can ask himself if the people, after listening to his homily, can say with the two disciples on the road to Emmaus: "Did not our hearts burn within us while he talked to us on the road, while he opened to us the Scriptures?" (Lk 24:32).

Let no priest suggest that he does not have the time. A quarter of an hour a day is not too much. There is always time for what is considered a priority. The priest can ask himself how much time he dedicates each day to newspapers, to the television, and to the computer, not to mention conversation that is not really of the highest quality or importance. No doubt, the news media are useful for keeping us updated on what is happening in the world so that we can present the Word of God in a way more related to what the people of today are experiencing. But who will deny that part of what the mass media tell us in the morning becomes debatable or is "clarified" at midday, while in the evening it is found in part either mistaken or not so useful! On the other hand, "the word of our God will stand for ever" (Is 40:8; cf. 1 Pet 1:25), and "Jesus Christ is the same yesterday and today and forever" (Heb 13:8).

Pope John Paul II insists: "The priest ought to be the first 'believer' in the word, while being fully aware that the words of his ministry are not 'his,' but those of the One who sent him. He is not the master of the word, but its servant. He is not the sole possessor of the word; in its regard he is in debt to the People of God."[11]

The 2008 Synod of Bishops asserted therefore that: "the Word of God is indispensable for the formation of the heart of a good pastor, of a good minister of the Word. . . . Priests, and in particular parish priests, are called to be nourished

---

[11] *Pastores Dabo Vobis* (March 25, 1992), 26.

every day with the Sacred Scriptures and to communicate them with wisdom and generosity to the faithful entrusted to their care." [12] "Your word is a lamp to my feet and a light to my path" (Ps 119:105).

5. Hopes Expressed by the 2008 Synod

In the undertaking to realize the hopes of the 2008 Synod of Bishops on the Word of God in the Life and Mission of the Church, the contribution of priests and bishops is of special significance. They occupy in the Church a ministry of crucial importance. They can, and should, take steps to help the whole Church enrich herself with what that Synod has contributed, and it is much.

The Holy Father expressed the following hope in his Christmas address to the Roman Curia on December 22, 2008:

> Now we hope that the experiences and the fruits of the Synod may have a constructive influence on the life of the Church: on our personal relationship with the Sacred Scriptures, on their interpretation in the liturgy and catechesis, as well as in scientific research, so that the Bible will not remain a Word from the past, but that its vitality and timeliness will be appreciated and brought to light against the vast horizon of its fullness of meaning. [13]

Diligent attention to Holy Scripture every day will not fail, in the long run, to bring many blessings to the Church. The prophet Isaiah in the first Reading of the Mass of this Tuesday of the First Week of Lent assures us: "For as the

[12] Prop. 31.

[13] Benedict XVI, address, December 22, 2008, *L'Osservatore Romano*, weekly English edition, January 7, 2009, p. 11.

rain and the snow come down from heaven, and do not return there but water the earth, . . . so shall my word be that goes forth from my mouth; it shall not return to me empty" (Is 55:10–11).

6. The Priest, Lover of Good Catholic Books

After the Bible, it is expected that the priest or the bishop will maintain good contact with good Catholic books. One thinks, for example, of documents of the Magisterium, such as the sixteen documents of the Second Vatican Council in our time; encyclicals and apostolic letters of the Holy Father; documents of the various offices of the Pope in the Roman Curia; publications from bishops; and writings of the best Catholic theologians or spiritual masters. People with a more scholarly background will be able to add the writings of the Fathers of the Church and the riches of theological masters recognized in the history of the Church.

Here it is not superfluous to mention the important service offered by good Catholic book shops in diocesan centers, in big cities, and also in parishes, according to local possibilities. The people of God should not have to make a long journey in order to find a place where they can buy the Bible in a properly approved translation, a missal, devotional books, the lives of the saints, Rosaries, and other devotional objects that promote the practice of our faith.

"The word of God is living and active, sharper than any two-edged sword" (Heb 4:12). The priest should love this word, meditate on it, and live it. May the Blessed Virgin Mary intercede for us, she who is the first of "those who hear the word of God and keep it" (Lk 11:28; cf. also Lk 2:19, 51).

VIII

THE PRIEST MEETS AND
FOLLOWS JESUS IN THE CHURCH

The priest who wants to meet Jesus and follow him finds him in the Church.

1. The Church, the Mystical Body of Christ

The Church is the communion of the baptized with Christ as their Head. She is the house of God, the family of God, the holy temple of God, the new Jerusalem, the Spouse of the Lamb. She is the Mystical Body of Christ, which does not get separated from Christ. The close union between Christ and his Church is thus described by the Second Vatican Council:

> The Head of this Body is Christ. He is the image of the invisible God and in Him all things came into being. He is before all creatures and in Him all things hold together. He is the head of the Body which is the Church. He is the beginning, the firstborn from the dead, that in all things He might have the first place (cf. Col 1:15–18). By the greatness of His power He rules the things in heaven and the things on earth, and with His all-surpassing perfection and way of acting He fills the whole body with the riches of His glory (cf. Eph 1:18–23).[1]

[1] *Lumen Gentium* (November 21, 1964), 7.

In the short Reading at Lauds on this Wednesday of the First Week of Lent, the Lord God says to the chosen people of the Old Testament: "For you are a people holy to the LORD your God; the LORD your God has chosen you to be a people for his own possession, out of all the peoples that are on the face of the earth" (Deut 7:6). This people is a symbol of the Church, the Mystical Body of Christ, the new people of God.

The patrimony, the inheritance, and the vocation of this people are beautiful, exceptional. The Council lists them. This messianic people has as its head Christ, "who was put to death for our trespasses and raised for our justification" (Rom 4:25). It has as its heritage the dignity and freedom of the children of God, in whose hearts the Holy Spirit dwells as in his temple. It has as its law the new commandment to love as Christ loved us (cf. Jn 13:34). And finally, it has as its goal the Kingdom of God, which has been begun by God himself on earth. Established by Christ as a fellowship of life, charity, and truth, this people is also used by him as an instrument for the redemption of all; and as the light of the world and the salt of the earth (cf. Mt 5:13–16), it is sent forth into the whole world.[2]

2. Faith in the Church

This Church has divine and human elements. The human elements can sometimes fall short. This has at times happened in the last two thousand years.

In the Credo, we profess: "I believe in one, holy, catholic, and apostolic Church." This is the Church that our beloved Savior, after his Resurrection, handed over to Peter

[2] Cf. ibid., 9.

to be shepherded, commissioning him and the other Apostles, and through them their successors, to diffuse and govern her until the end of the world. This is the Church that has the guarantee of Christ and the assistance of the Holy Spirit, so that the gates of hell may not prevail against her (cf. Mt 16:18). Jesus did not guarantee that no member of the Church would ever fall short, or even that the Church could not be so persecuted that she would almost disappear in a particular place. But he did promise that the Church in the world will remain until he should come again in glory.

Moreover, when we say *Church*, we do not mean just the Pope and the bishops in communion with him. We mean all the people of God: the lay faithful, who form more than 98 percent of the Church; the clerics; and the men and women in the consecrated life. Every member of the Church is called to holiness. It might happen that some members are indeed not holy, but this does not mean that they cease to be members of the Church.

It is important that we believe in *this* Church, not in an imaginary Church that does not exist. We do not deny that scandals take place, and it is worse when the bad example comes from clerics or consecrated people. But we do not for this reason lose our faith in the Church or our love for her. Scandals should rather urge us to do penance and to live holy lives. Pope Paul VI wrote in the Apostolic Constitution on the Revision of Indulgences, on January 1, 1967, that by a hidden and merciful mystery of the divine will, a supernatural solidarity exists between people. As a consequence, the sin of one person does harm to other persons, just as the holiness of one helps the others.[3]

---

[3] *Indulgentiarum Doctrina* (January 1, 1967), 4.

3. The Priest loves the Church

It seems almost superfluous to say that the priest should love the Church. He shares her joys and sorrows, her projects and challenges. As a priest he is calm and contented, even when his priest colleague, or some parishioner, or his bishop, or even himself if he is honest, is not as holy as he should be.

The priest who loves the Church does not lament and criticize the Church from the first of January to the thirty-first of December. A child who loves his mother or his family does not cut her or the family to pieces on the pages of the newspaper or over the waves of the radio or the television. There exist very different ways for a child or other member of the family to seek to remedy embarrassing situations. If a priest criticized the Church, he would be cutting off the branch on which he were sitting. It would be a sign that something was wrong with his interior life. Free speech in the Church is very different from that in the world and can be exercised in several ways. "No one can have God as Father who does not have the Church as Mother."[4] We can meditate on the homily given by the Holy Father on February 20, 2009, during his visit to the community of the Pontifical Major Seminary of Rome. He commented on Galatians 5:13–16, saying that destructive criticism in the Church cannot be approved.[5]

As can be seen, all of this applies even more to the bishop. He is an image of Christ, the Spouse of the Church. The bishop's ring indicates his mystical marriage with the Church, with the particular Church or diocese confided to him.

---

[4] St. Cyprian, *De Catholicae unitate Ecclesiae*, 6; PL 4:519.
[5] Cf. Benedict XVI, homily, *L'Osservatore Romano*, February 22, 2009, p. 8.

4. Love for the Church in the Roman Curia

A priest or bishop who is at the service of the Holy Father in the Roman Curia can show his love for the Church in various ways. Some examples include working with a team spirit; knowing how to sacrifice oneself when the public does not know who has worked more on a document; having a spirit of solidarity when a mistake has been made; keeping official secrets where this is necessary; coming to the help of colleagues who feel themselves forgotten or unappreciated; avoiding the exaggerations of bureaucracy, which puts papers before the people behind the papers; maintaining a vision of the universality of the Church, which is reflected also in different nationalities from which the staff come; and radiating gratuity and joy in daily work and in the reception of visitors and the answering of telephone calls. Considering the excellent service rendered by many officials in the Roman Curia, service often hidden from the eyes of the public, some of these officials could be proposed for canonization, except that they are still on this side of the grave!

I would like to mention in particular the important service rendered in the Roman Curia by receiving the bishops who come to the various offices, especially for the *ad limina* visits. The bishops, after all, are the shepherds whom the Holy Spirit "has made . . . guardians, to feed the Church of the Lord which he obtained with his own blood" (Acts 20:28).

All of this is rather demanding. But love is demanding.

5. Service as Love

The love of the priest for the Church shows itself in service. The person who loves feels privileged to be able to serve the loved one. In the case of the priest, it is a question of love for the Church, the Mystical Body of Christ. The priest could ask himself whether it is his joy to be at the service of this Church. Does he resist the temptation to use the Church or her structures for self-promotion? Can he truly apply to himself the advice of his Master Jesus: "When you have done all that is commanded you, say, 'We are unworthy servants; we have only done what is our duty'" (Lk 17:10)?

6. The Service of Administration

One aspect of the ministry of the priest, and much more that of the diocesan bishop, is the service of administration. It is not acceptable that a bishop should defend himself by saying that he is the practical type and does not love paperwork in the office. The reality is that the Church is a visible body that has grown in numbers since the days of Saint Peter. Every diocese has many things to organize: the appointment of priests to various offices, the study of the dossiers of each seminarian long before ordination to avoid last-moment dramatic decisions, the granting of faculties and indults, the maintenance of correspondence with the bishops' conference and the Roman Curia, and contacts with the civil authorities. Moreover, there are the religious and the lay faithful who have the right to receive attention in their various institutes and associations; there are commissions and professional groups that should have chaplains assigned to them; and there is the vast field of the mass media.

Effectively to carry out all this and much more, the bishop needs an efficient diocesan office. Clarifying ideas, deciding on priorities, doing timely research on problems and challenges, making decisions that cannot be postponed indefinitely—all of this weighs on the bishop and his co-workers. If letters received remain for a long time without an answer, if documents get lost in the office because of a poor filing system or because of inefficient staff, or if the diocese has the reputation of not responding to questionnaires, then we cannot see how such a bishop can say that he loves the Church!

All of this can be applied, *mutatis mutandis*, to a bishop or priest of the Roman Curia, to a parish priest, or to a priest or bishop with special ecclesiastical assignments.

7. Love for the Church through a Holy Life

A priest or bishop who leads a holy life shows great love for Christ and the Church. Let us say a word on life according to the Gospel in chastity, poverty, and obedience, following the model set for us by Jesus.

A priest or bishop loves the Church if he lives celibacy not as a mere ecclesiastical discipline but as pastoral charity for motives that are Christological, theological, and ecclesiological. Spiritual fatherhood of the priest in the Church demands, explains, and justifies the sacrifices that celibacy involves, together with the joy that fidelity brings. Only thus can the priest inspire colleagues, religious, spouses, and single lay faithful to live chastity according to each person's vocation.

Even if the priest or bishop has not taken a vow of poverty, he is expected to follow Jesus in evangelical simplicity, to be unattached to earthly goods, and to show solidarity with the needy. He should take care not to seek prestige with money or lifestyle or to subtly desire an easy life segregated from the common man.

The priest at his ordination promises obedience to the bishop, and the latter at his episcopal ordination promises obedience to the Successor of Saint Peter. Much faith is needed, together with love for the Church and a good dosage of humility, if the spirit of obedience is to be lived. It is a great source of suffering for the Church when a priest, or even more so a bishop, becomes part of the problem instead of part of the solution for a harmonious apostolate in the Church. A consideration that can help the priest (or bishop) to appreciate even more the value and the importance of sacerdotal obedience in the Church is the following. God has made the priest a depositary, in the Church, of the treasure of salvation that Jesus has won on the Cross—his Word; the sacraments, especially the Most Holy Eucharist; and the community of believers in Christ—all for the purpose of facilitating communion with the Father. For this reason, the priest must administer these goods faithfully, in complete and sincere submission to the Church from which he received them. And this Church is the Body of Christ. She is the Spouse of Christ. Love for this Church includes obedience in faith and trust. And a person who loves Christ must necessarily love the Church.

8. Interest in Pastoral Concerns of the Church

The priest who follows Jesus shows great interest in the different concerns of the Church. Let us mention some of them.

In one country after another, marriage and the family are

under attack by well-organized groups. Depending on the vaious cultural areas, there are people who denigrate marriage, who commercialize women and children, and who do not consider children a gift from God to the spouses. The falling birth rate in these countries has its effect on the traditional Christian culture and on the fall in vocations to the priesthood and the religious life.

Relativism and moral laxity raise their ugly heads in the press, on the radio and television, in parliaments, and even in intergovernmental assemblies. All the while, the proper Christian education of children is rendered more difficult for the parents.

Persecution of the Church takes many forms in our times. There is the practical deprivation of the right to religious freedom. There is the killing of missionaries or simply of believers in Christ. There is discrimination against Christians in society. Sometimes one can speak of "Christianophobia". We could continue; but there is no need.

The priest who meets and follows Jesus finds him in the Church. The three magi, after a long journey and search, found Jesus with the Virgin Mary, his Mother. The priest will not fail to pray to the Blessed Virgin Mary, Mother of priests and Mother of the Church, to obtain for him great faith and love for Jesus in the Church, his Mystical Body.

IX

THE PRIEST MEETS JESUS IN
OTHER PERSONS IN THE CHURCH

The ministry of the priest or bishop puts him in relationship with other persons in the Church and outside of her. He is not an isolated operator. "God . . . does not make men holy and save them merely as individuals, without bond or link between one another. Rather has it pleased Him to bring men together as one people, a people which acknowledges Him in truth and serves Him in holiness."[1] It is therefore useful for us to meditate on how the priest meets Jesus in the other persons in the Church—bishops, presbyters, religious, and lay faithful—and how harmony is necessary among Church personnel.

1. Bishops among Themselves

A bishop at his appointment and ordination becomes associated and bound with the whole episcopal body through the Successor of Saint Peter. In the rite of ordination the candidate promises to take steps to build up the Body of Christ, the Church, and to remain in the unity of that Body together with the order of bishops under the authority of the Pope. As Pope Benedict said to the bishops of Kenya on

[1] Vatican Council II, *Lumen Gentium* (November 21, 1964), 9.

73

November 19, 2007, "The collegial nature of the episcopal ministry traces its origins to the twelve Apostles, called
together by Christ and given the task of proclaiming the
Gospel and making disciples of all nations."[2]

That is the sacramental foundation that motivates the collaboration of a bishop with other bishops in the spirit of collegiality and in the disposition to seek together with them
solutions to problems and challenges that go beyond the
frontiers of a diocese, without taking away the right and
responsibility of the diocesan bishop to teach. Collegiality
also fosters a bishop's obedience to the See of Peter, a spirit
of collaboration, openness to offer his best priests from the
diocese for the direct service of the Holy Father, and inter-
dicasterial collaboration within the Roman Curia.

The spirit that should animate and nourish collegiality
manifests itself in various ways. A sense of humility that the
individual, even if he be the superior, does not necessarily
understand all sides of a question and does not possess all
the answers; the recognition of our belonging to something
bigger than ourselves, which is the Church; appreciation
of the demands of true fraternity—these are some of the
manifestations of the authentic spirit of collegiality. A consequence is the readiness to listen patiently to the position
of the other, together with the openness to modify or even
entirely change one's position when this becomes really necessary in the light of more complete information. The practice of collegiality ensures freshness and almost youthfulness
of spirit even as the years roll by.

---

[2] *Ad limina* visit address, *L'Osservatore Romano*, November 19–20, 2007,
p. 7.

2. The Bishop with His Priests

The rite of ordination of presbyters refers to priests in the following terms: faithful cooperators of the order of bishops, co-workers of whom we have need, faithful dispensers of (divine) mysteries, and ministers of the second priestly grade.[3]

The Second Vatican Council sees priests as "co-workers of the episcopal order". "Through the ministry of the priests, the spiritual sacrifice of the faithful is made perfect in union with the sacrifice of Christ . . . the only mediator."[4] "All presbyters, both diocesan and religious, participate in and exercise with the bishop the one priesthood of Christ and are thereby constituted prudent cooperators of the episcopal order. . . . Diocesan priests who are incardinated or attached to a particular church . . . form one presbytery and one family whose father is the bishop."[5] Priests are friends and spiritual sons of the bishop.

The spirit that should reign in relations between the bishop and his priests follows from this teaching. In particular, the bishop should know his priests well, with their talents and particular situations. He should in a special way be near to those who find themselves in some difficulty. All of this can apply to the Roman Curia.

[3] Cf. *Pontificale Romanum*, De Ordinatione Presbyterorum.
[4] *Presbyterorum Ordinis* (December 7, 1965), 2.
[5] *Christus Dominus* (October 28, 1965), 28.

3. Consecrated People

The rite of religious profession and of the consecration of other persons in the Church shows how precious to the Church is the patrimony of the consecrated life. The Second Vatican Council does not hesitate to declare: "Thus, the state which is constituted by the profession of the evangelical counsels, though it is not the hierarchical structure of the Church, nevertheless, undeniably belongs to its life and holiness."[6]

The priest or bishop should know well the constitutions of the orders or religious congregations in his territory, encourage consecrated persons, preach vocations to people living in this state, and not forget to give attention in a special way to monasteries, some of which could be very poor indeed.

4. The Lay Faithful

When considering the vocation and the mission of the lay faithful in the Church and in the world, we shall dwell longer on relations between clerics and the lay faithful, taking into account the fact that many misunderstandings exist between clerics and the laity.

The bishop should be the foremost person to help the lay faithful, clerics, and religious see clearly the theological basis of the lay apostolate and the reasons for its necessity. The Second Vatican Council is rather clear: "The laity derive the right and duty to the apostolate from their union with Christ the head; incorporated into Christ's Mystical Body through Baptism and strengthened by the power of

[6] *Lumen Gentium*, 44.

the Holy Spirit through Confirmation, they are assigned to
the apostolate by the Lord Himself. They are consecrated
for the royal priesthood and the holy people. . . . On all
Christians therefore is laid the preeminent responsibility of
working to make the divine message of salvation known and
accepted by all men throughout the world."[7]

The apostolate specific to the lay faithful is the Christian-
ization or evangelization of the secular order from within. It
is for the laity to evangelize the family; recreation and work;
science and the arts; technology; industry; culture and the
mass media; and politics and international relations.[8] When
they do all of this, they are not "helping" the clerics but are
rather living their Baptism, Confirmation, and Holy Communion.

A capable parish priest or an efficient bishop has nothing
to fear from well-informed and capable laypeople. The contrary is the case. Everyone has his own area of apostolate.
No star is a threat to other stars. There is enough room for
all of them in the constellation of creation. "For their pastors", says the Second Vatican Council, "know how much
the laity contribute to the welfare of the entire Church.
They also know that they were not ordained by Christ to
take upon themselves alone the entire salvific mission of the
Church toward the world. On the contrary they understand
that it is their noble duty to shepherd the faithful and to recognize their ministries and charisms, so that all according
to their proper roles may cooperate in this common undertaking with one mind."[9]

This directive of the Council is of great importance. And
if some cleric still has any remaining doubt on what he might

[7] *Apostolican Actuositatem* (November 18, 1965), 3.
[8] Ibid., 2, 7.
[9] *Lumen Gentium*, 30.

consider the risk of too much freedom and initiative for the laity, *Lumen Gentium* returns to the same idea in paragraph 37 with words a little more incisive: "Let the spiritual shepherds recognize and promote the dignity as well as the responsibility of the layity in the Church. . . . Let them encourage lay people so that they may undertake tasks on their own initiative. . . . However, let the shepherds respectfully acknowledge that just freedom which belongs to everyone in this earthly city."

Gaudium et Spes urges the lay faithful to take on their proper responsibilities: "Let the layman not imagine that his pastors are always such experts, that to every problem which arises, however complicated, they can readily give him a concrete solution, or even that such is their mission. Rather, enlightened by Christian wisdom and giving close attention to the teaching authority of the Church, let the layman take on his own distinctive role."[10]

The priest, therefore, should do his part: celebrate the sacraments, preach, continue with good ongoing theological formation, and not assume the attitude of a clericalist. The lay faithful, on their part, should be well formed in the social doctrine of the Church, be ready to take initiative when necessary, be open to harmony and obedience in the Church, and not assume the attitude of a laicist.

There is no doubt that discretion is needed. The Council does not ignore this point. It says that the one who has received a charism should exercise it for the good of people and in building up the Church in communion with his brothers in Christ, above all with the pastors. The pastors, continues the Council, "must make a judgment about the true nature and proper use of these gifts, not in order to

[10] Vatican Council II, *Gaudium et Spes* (December 7, 1965), 43.

extinguish the Spirit, but to test all things and hold fast to what is good (cf. 1 Thess 5:12, 19, 21)."[11]

5. Appointments and Collaboration

For services in the diocese and in the Roman Curia, or in other units of the Church, it is obvious that the superiors have to make appointments to the various offices. Consultation is very useful. A priest who considers that some grave harm could happen to him or to the Church, or to society, if he were to accept an appointment assigned to him has the freedom and even the responsibility to bring to light all his reasons to his superiors. But there is eventually a time when dialogue is over and obedience begins. A priest who lives a life of faith knows that Divine Providence will not fail to protect and bless the one who accepts the mission assigned to him and strives to make it succeed, with all his gifts of nature and grace. Such a person never presents himself as martyred by his superiors!

Rather unpleasant is the action of the person who allows himself to be overcome by the temptation to look for someone who knows someone who knows someone else who can try to influence his superiors so that they make the type of decision that he likes. Such a person might even try to please his superiors by giving advice, not exactly as he sees the situation, but rather according to what he believes will please his superiors. Such a person is never sure that he is doing God's will, even when he succeeds in obtaining the desired appointment.

On his part, the superior should not be discouraged from asking advice, even though we all know that consultation

---

[11] *Apostolicam Actuositatem*, 3; cf. *Presbyterorum Ordinis*, 9.

does not relieve the superior from the responsibility of finally making the necessary decision. Saint Benedict directs the abbot to call together the whole family when in the monastery it is necessary to examine an important problem: "Call all to a consultation, because often the Lord reveals the best solution to the youngest."[12]

6. Encourage the Personnel

In all offices of the Church—parish, diocese, Roman Curia, or other—it is of great importance that workers receive encouragement from their superiors. Everybody is good at something. No one is good and capable in everything. It is the duty of the superior to find out where a person is most gifted and to seek, as far as possible, to assign the person duties in that area. Encouragement and appreciation increase productivity in all of us.

Weakness, carelessness, and even laziness will never entirely disappear. The superior cannot approve of these failings or pretend not to notice them. But the climate in every office should be one of calm, where praise is given where this is deserved, suggestions are listened to even from the youngest, and there is a clear and gentle way of showing disapproval. In the first Servant Song, the prophet Isaiah says:

> He will not cry or lift up his voice,
>   or make it heard in the street;
> a bruised reed he will not break,
>   and a dimly burning wick he will not quench;
> he will faithfully bring forth justice. (Is 42:2–3)

[12] *Rule of Saint Benedict*, chap. 3.

No one is always wrong. Even a broken clock is right twice a day. And Saint Francis de Sales says that we can catch more flies with a spoonful of honey than with a whole barrel of vinegar.

7. Rivalry and Jealousy

Because of the consequences of original sin, we cannot completely exclude rivalry and jealousy in interpersonal relations, even at various levels in the Church. The Gospel does not hide from us the fact that John said to Jesus: "Master, we saw a man casting out demons in your name, and we forbade him, because he does not follow with us." But Jesus did not approve of this line of conduct: "Do not forbid him; for he that is not against you is for you" (Lk 9:49–50).

To pastoral workers who are tempted by rivalry or jealousy, one can propose the example of Saints Basil and Gregory of Nazianzen. Each of them rejoiced because of the success of the other as if it were his own. Each wanted to promote the other, not himself. The Reading in the Divine Office of January 2 from a sermon of Saint Gregory of Nazianzen is full of instruction.

The person who allows himself to be overcome by the temptation to rivalry or jealousy should reflect on the fact that one could then begin to think that he is now preaching and projecting himself, and no longer Jesus Christ.

Writing to the Philippians, Saint Paul shows us how to conquer the temptation to rivalry. Some, writes Saint Paul, "proclaim Christ out of partisanship, not sincerely but thinking to afflict me in my imprisonment." Then he makes the vital comment: "What then? Only that in every way, whether in pretense or in truth, Christ is proclaimed; and in that I rejoice" (Phil 1:17–18).

Let us conclude by thanking God that in the Church there are many mansions, that everyone has some contribution to make, and that the success of one is the joy of all. Saint Paul comes to our aid: "There are varieties of gifts, but the same Spirit; and there are varieties of service, but the same Lord; and there are varieties of working, but it is the same God who inspires them all in every one" (1 Cor 12:4–6). Therefore, "Bear one another's burdens, and so fulfil the law of Christ" (Gal 6:2).

X

THE PRIEST EVANGELIZING WITH ZEAL

The priest who meets Jesus and follows him is intensely interested and involved in the evangelizing work of the Church. It could not be otherwise.

1. The Church Is Missionary by Her Very Nature

The pilgrim Church on earth is by her very nature missionary because she takes her origin from the mission of the Son and the mission of the Holy Spirit. It is God who, out of his completely gratuitous mercy, calls us to communicate in life and glory with him.[1] In Christ we are called to become the new people of God. Having accomplished the work of our redemption by his life and especially by the paschal mystery of his suffering, death, and Resurrection, Jesus sends his Church to bring the Gospel to the whole world. On the Apostles gathered with the Most Blessed Virgin Mary, he sends the Holy Spirit.

Jesus gives his Church a universal mandate: "You shall receive power when the Holy Spirit has come upon you; and you shall be my witnesses in Jerusalem and in all Judea and Samaria and to the end of the earth" (Acts 1:8).

[1] Cf. Vatican Council II, *Ad Gentes* (December 7, 1965), 2.

2. Religious Statistics

The priest or bishop cannot remain indifferent in the face of the fact that in the world today Catholics constitute only 17.4 percent of all humanity. All other Christians comprise about 15.6 percent. That means that all who believe in Christ make up one-third of the world's population. And that figure includes Christians who do not remember when they last set foot in a church building!

Muslims make up 19.2 percent, Hindus 13 percent, and Buddhists 7 percent. Then there are people of a great many other religions: Jews, followers of traditional natural religions, Sikhs, Jainists, Shintoists, and others. And there are millions of persons without a clear religion, or even those who by ideology deny the existence of God.[2]

For all these people Jesus died on the Cross.

Within the Church, there is preoccupation because many Catholics do not come to Sunday Mass or the sacrament of Penance often; entire populations are becoming gradually dechristianized and have need of reevangelization; religious ignorance is growing; and in some cultures the number of vocations to the priesthood and the religious life is diminishing. On the positive side, the number of Catholics in Africa is on the increase. The growth is to the tune of 6,708 percent between the years 1900 and 2000, when the figure passed from 1.9 million to 130 million.[3]

There is also the great challenge of the division between Christians and the urgency of ecumenism.

[2] Cf. David Barrett, George T. Kurian, and Todd M. Johnson, eds., *World Christian Encyclopaedia: A Comparative Survey of Churches and Religions in the Modern World*, 2nd ed. (Oxford: Oxford University Press, 2001).

[3] Cf. zenit.org, June 18, 2007.

3. Zeal for Evangelization

The priest or bishop cannot remain unmoved in the face of the above facts. He should have the fire of desire to bring Christ to others so that they may have life in abundance and not remain hungry or thirsty (cf. Jn 6:35). Zeal is this burning desire, accompanied by action, so that all may know the one true God and Jesus Christ whom he has sent (cf. Jn 17:3). As we have already noted in our reflections, Jesus is the one and only Savior for all humanity. There is salvation only in him (cf. Jn 4:42; Acts 4:12). Saint Paul burned with desire and initiatives to propagate this Good News of salvation in Jesus Christ: "To them God chose to make known how great among the Gentiles are the riches of the glory of this mystery, which is Christ in you, the hope of glory. Him we proclaim, warning every man and teaching every man in all wisdom, that we may present every man mature in Christ. For this I toil, striving with all the energy which he mightily inspires within me" (Col 1:27–29).

Every priest should participate in the evangelizing activity of the Church, including the *mission ad gentes*, as explained by *Ad Gentes* and *Redemptoris Missio*. The priest should not hide behind slogans such as "respect for the consciences of others" or "avoid being judgmental" or "salvific elements in other religions" in order to finish up by doing precious little, or nothing at all, to share the Catholic faith with persons who freely welcome it and listen to it. The love of Christ should possess him and urge him on (cf. 2 Cor 5:14), so that he can with truth say with Saint Paul: "I count everything as loss because of the surpassing worth of knowing Christ Jesus my Lord" (Phil 3:8). "Woe to me if I do not preach the gospel" (1 Cor 9:16).

4. Witness of a Pentecostal

Sometimes it can be useful for us to hear what people who are not Catholics think of the Catholic Church. Let us hear what the historian Thomas Babington Macaulay (1800–1859), an Evangelical Protestant from England, wrote in the *Edinburgh Review* as far back as 1840, almost 170 years ago. He does not hide his admiration for the Catholic Church. However, I believe that he was not particularly considering the role of Jesus Christ or of the Holy Spirit. Rather, he seems to see the Catholic Church purely as an institution that has outlasted all others. Here is his witness:

> There is not, and there never was on this earth, a work of human policy so well deserving of examination as the Roman Catholic Church. The history of that Church joins together the two great ages of human civilization. No other institution is left standing which carries the mind back to the times when the smoke of sacrifice rose from the Pantheon, and when camelopards and tigers bounded in the Flavian amphitheatre. The proudest royal houses are but of yesterday, when compared with the line of the Supreme Pontiffs. That line we trace back in an unbroken series, from the Pope who crowned Napoleon in the nineteenth century to the Pope who crowned Pepin in the eighth; and far beyond the time of Pepin the august dynasty extends, till it is lost in the twilight of fable. The republic of Venice came next in antiquity. But the republic of Venice was modern when compared with the Papacy; and the republic of Venice is gone, and the Papacy remains. The Papacy remains, not in decay, not a mere antique, but full of life and youthful vigour. The Catholic Church is still sending forth to the farthest ends of the world missionaries as zealous as those who landed in Kent with Augustine, and still confronting hostile kings

with the same spirit with which she confronted Attila. The number of her children is greater than in any former age. Her acquisitions in the New World have more than compensated for what she has lost in the Old. Her spiritual ascendency extends over the vast countries which lie between the plains of the Missouri and Cape Horn, countries which a century hence, may not improbably contain a population as large as that which now inhabits Europe. The members of her communion are certainly not fewer than a hundred and fifty millions; and it will be difficult to show that all other Christian sects united amount to a hundred and twenty millions. Nor do we see any sign which indicates that the term of her long dominion is approaching. She saw the commencement of all the governments and of all the ecclesiastical establishments that now exist in the world; and we feel no assurance that she is not destined to see the end of them all. She was great and respected before the Saxon had set foot on Britain, before the Frank had passed the Rhine, when Grecian eloquence still flourished at Antioch, when idols were still worshipped in the temple of Mecca. And she may still exist in undiminished vigour when some traveller from New Zealand shall, in the midst of a vast solitude, take his stand on a broken arch of London Bridge to sketch the ruins of St. Paul's.[4]

5. The Sacred Liturgy Evangelizes

The sacred liturgy is celebrated for the glory of God and for the salvation of the world. Well celebrated, the public worship of the Church is also catechesis and evangelization.

[4] Thomas Babington Macaulay, review of *The Ecclesiastical and Political History of the Popes of Rome, during the Sixteenth and Seventeenth Centureis*, by Leopold Ranke, in *Critical and Historical Essays, Contributed to the "Edinburgh Review"* (London: Longman, Brown, Green, and Longmans, 1850), 535–36.

It puts before us the transcendence of God and our duty to adore him.

In particular, the solemnity of the Epiphany celebrates the manifestation of Christ to the nations and therefore the urgency of the missionary activity of the Church. On the last Sunday of October, the Church celebrates World Mission Sunday in order to draw our attention to the necessity of the preaching of the Gospel. There are two beautiful votive Masses for the Evangelization of Peoples in the *Roman Missal*. In the rites of ordination of presbyters and bishops, the Church insists on the importance of maintaining the integrity of the deposit of faith according to tradition; of celebrating with devotion and fidelity the mysteries of Christ; of carrying out with dignity and wisdom the ministry of the Word; of imploring the divine mercy on the people; and of building up the Body of Christ, which is the Church.[5]

6. Catechesis and Religious Education

The zealous priest appreciates the urgency of ensuring catechesis and religious education that are clearly Catholic for his people, beginning with the children. We should thank God for the work of the many priests, religious, and catechists who are engaged in this apostolate. And we should thank the Holy Father for the systematic catechesis he gives in the weekly Wednesday general audiences. This sends a strong message to the whole Church.

The teaching of the Catholic faith in schools—primary, secondary, and tertiary—meets with some obstacles in many countries, especially in the public schools. The local Church cannot afford to underestimate the importance of the ques-

[5] Cf. *Roman Pontifical.*

tion. As a son of the missionary Church, I hereby pay tribute to the missionaries and the catechists who have promoted religious formation in school and out of school. This is also the occasion to thank the Congregation for the Evangelization of Peoples for all that it does to support catechists in the missions, particularly in their initial and ongoing formation and in guaranteeing a just pay for them, together with provisions for their old age.

The priest and bishop cannot complain of a lack of documents for catechesis and religious education. After the basic books of the Bible and the *Roman Missal*, the Church has three excellent volumes: the *Catechism of the Catholic Church*, the *Compendium of the Catechism of the Catholic Church*, and the *Compendium of the Social Doctrine of the Church*. No other religious family in the world is endowed with tools of such excellent quality. Diocesan book shops should be great propagators of these treasures.

7. Other Diocesan Initiatives

Every diocesan bishop, considering the command of the Lord: "Preach the gospel to the whole creation" (Mk 16:15), cannot avoid asking himself how his diocese "fosters the missions with care and attention".[6] What is being done to bring the Gospel to populations that have not yet received Christ? What initiatives are there in the diocese for contacting the followers of other religions and collaborating with them, even if they do not want to become Christians, as *Nostra Aetate* and *Dialogue and Proclamation* clearly indicate?[7]

[6] Vatican Council II, *Lumen Gentium* (November 21, 1964), 16.
[7] Vatican Council II, *Nostra Aetate* (October 28, 1964); Pontifical Council for Inter-religious Dialogue, *Dialogue and Proclamation* (May 19, 1991).

Is there a program to bring financial and other help from the richer parishes to the poorer ones in the same diocese? And within the same country, what measures does the diocese adopt for the evangelization of the less-christianized areas? Does the bishop succeed in convincing some of his diocesan priests to go to work as *Fidei Donum* priests in other dioceses of the country or in other countries?[8]

How is the annual World Mission Sunday celebrated in the diocese? Are the religious congregations and orders that work in the diocese well placed in the diocesan apostolate? Is there a ceremony organized in the cathedral for departing missionaries or for those returning home on holidays or in a permanent way?

What is being done in the diocese for the reevangelization of persons who have lost contact with the Church?

Pope John Paul II spoke of a new evangelization, new not of course in its content but rather in its methods and expressions and in the zeal with which it is pursued.[9] The use of the press, radio, television, internet, and their derivatives for the work of evangelization is not an option in today's world. The question, rather, is: What places has the diocese reached in the use of these modern media?

When Jesus chased the traders out of the temple, "his disciples remembered that it was written, 'Zeal for your house will consume me' " (Jn 2:17). May it be true that this comment be made of every priest, every bishop!

---

[8] Cf. Pius XII, *Fidei Donum* (April 21, 1957); Vatican Council II, *Presbyterorum Ordinis* (December 7, 1965), 10; Vatican Council II, *Ad Gentes*.

[9] Cf. Address to the Assembly of CELAM [Consejo Episcopal Latinoamericano (the Latin American Episcopal Conference)], on March 9, 1983; Inaugural Address on the Occasion of the Fourth General Conference of the Latin American Episcopate, October 12, 1992.

XI

THE PRIEST PRAYS

If the priest intends to meet Jesus and follow him closely, he has to pray. He will give attention to communal prayer and to personal prayer and apply himself with even greater diligence to liturgical prayer.

1. Following the Example and Teaching of Jesus

Our Savior Jesus Christ teaches us that we must pray, and he teaches us how to pray. The evangelists often report that during his public ministry he prayed. On many occasions, Jesus sought solitude in order to pray. Sometimes it was on a mountain. Other times it was by night. At his baptism by John in the river Jordan, Jesus prayed (cf. Lk 3:21); before choosing the twelve Apostles, he passed the whole night in prayer and communication with his eternal Father (cf. Lk 6:12). Jesus prayed for Peter, that his faith might not fall short (cf. Lk 22:32). He prayed at his own transfiguration (cf. Lk 9:28–29); when the Greeks wanted to see him (cf. Jn 12:27–28); on the Mount of Olives (cf. Mt 26:39–42; Lk 22:39–44); and on the Cross (cf. Mt 27:46).

Some explicit prayers of Jesus have been documented by the evangelists. Here are three great prayers: when Jesus praises the Father for having revealed the secrets of the Kingdom to the little ones (cf. Mt 11:25–27; Lk 10:21–23); before raising Lazarus from the dead (cf. Jn 11:41–42); and during the Last Supper, in his long and exceptional priestly prayer for his chosen ones (cf. Jn 17). These three prayers merit quiet meditation.

Jesus prayed so much that on one occasion one of his disciples said to him: "Lord, teach us to pray, as John taught his disciples" (Lk 11:1). And Jesus taught them the masterly Our Father.

Jesus the Master teaches us how to pray. We should first be reconciled with our brother if he has anything against us, and only then will God accept our offerings (cf. Mt 5:23–24). We should not use too many words (Mt 6:7). We should pray with faith and knock at the door with perseverance (cf. Lk 11:5–8). We should pray with humility like the publican and not like the Pharisee (cf. Lk 18:9–14). The eternal Father will give us another Paraclete who will remain with us, the Spirit of truth (cf. Jn 14:16–17). "In the Holy Spirit, Christian prayer is a communion of love with the Father, not only through Christ but also *in him*."[1]

Jesus prays to his Father. He teaches us to pray to God as children to their father. God is "our Father who art in heaven".

2. *Our Prayer Will Be Heard*

Jesus assures us that our prayer will be heard. In the Gospel of the Holy Mass for this Thursday of the First Week of Lent, he says to us: "Ask, and it will be given you; seek,

[1] *CCC* 2615 (emphasis in original).

and you will find; knock, and it will be opened to you. . . . If you then, who are evil, know how to give good gifts to your children, how much more will your Father who is in heaven give good things to those who ask him!" (Mt 7:7, 11).

In the short Reading at Lauds of this same day, Solomon at the dedication of the temple of Jerusalem prayed the Lord in the name of the chosen people: "Let your eyes be open to the supplication of your servant, and to the supplication of your people Israel, giving ear to them whenever they call to you. For you separated them from among all the peoples of the earth, to be your heritage" (1 Kings 8:52-53). So will God hear the prayer of the Church offered through his Son, under the impulse of the Holy Spirit.

3. The Priest's Participation in Community Prayers

The priest should not underestimate the importance of his participation in the community prayers of his people, such as are Eucharistic adoration, the *Via Crucis*, the Rosary, pilgrimages, processions, Marian devotions in May and October, and devotions in honor of the patron saints of the parish or diocese. When such exercises of popular devotion are directed by good theology, guided with wise liturgical discernment, and inspired by Holy Scripture, they can deeply enrich the Christian life. The priest or bishop will find considerable help in the *Directory on Popular Devotions and the Liturgy* issued by the Congregation for Divine Worship and the Discipline of the Sacraments in 2002.

Popular devotions, together with the sacred liturgy, educate the sentiments according to faith and reason and are helpful to people in various vocations: clerics, consecrated persons, and lay faithful.

4. Daily Mental Prayer

Among the various forms of personal prayer of the priest or bishop, daily mental prayer deserves special mention. The general advice is that it should last for at least half an hour. It is not to be reduced to spiritual reading, even of a biblical text, although such a reading is an excellent preparation for it.

The priest should resist the temptation to cut back on these moments dedicated to daily meeting with the Father, the Son, and the Holy Spirit. We are all agreed that quality is more important than quantity. But, all the same, quality requires some minimum quantity in which to adhere. Otherwise we might end up with sophism, because if the time for this mental prayer were progressively reduced, at the end only a few minutes would remain. If the priest were to defend himself by alleging that his many pastoral duties are the reason for the reduction of the time that he can afford to give to mental prayer each day, then it would not be unfair to ask him how much time he gives every day to the newspapers, the television, and the computer.

Proofs that the priest is probably neglecting his daily time with God in mental prayer could be the following: pastoral action becoming all the time more breakneck but with precious little fruit; defects of impatience, intolerance of others' opinions, and irritation in the face of things going against his desire; subtle self-seeking becoming all the time more evident; and celebration of Holy Mass, the Liturgy of the

Hours, and the rest of the liturgy lacking unction, devotion, and calm. These could be some of the lights flickering to indicate that the prayer life of the priest needs greater attention.

It could also happen that the priest is careless over daily mental prayer and other personal prayer because he is not convinced of any harm that happens to him because of this negligence. He thinks that he preaches well, is attentive to the faithful and gracious toward all, and gives a good example. In reality he is not aware of the deficiencies, often significant, in his ministry and in his spiritual life, precisely because he does not pray and does not put himself in the presence of the Lord. It is actually in his daily conversation with the Lord that he will discover the daily demands of faithfulness and the needed solutions (that is, those according to the Heart of Jesus) to the diverse challenges of the priestly ministry. There also he will discover defects in faith, hope, and charity. It is prayer that helps us to recognize our dependence on the Lord, without whom we can do nothing (cf. Jn 15:4-5)

5. Initiating His People into Personal Prayer

On the question of personal prayer, many Catholics need to go further. For many, to pray is to read or recite a prayer already composed. Certainly, the Our Father has no equal. And there are fixed and approved prayers like the Hail Mary; acts of faith, hope, and charity; and so forth. And there are excellent prayers composed by great saints like Thomas Aquinas, Bonaventure, Alphonsus Maria de Liguori, and Bernard. All of these prayers are very good.

Nevertheless, there is still need for personal prayer, in addition to prayers already composed by others. We need acts of adoration, love, thanksgiving, praise, reparation, and petition that well up from the heart of the individual and are directed toward God. Catholics have a real need to be introduced to such prayers and be helped to make them. One thinks, for example, of the hour of going to bed or rising, of a brief visit to the Most Blessed Sacrament, of the precious moments after the reception of Holy Communion, and of the opening and closing of meetings and gatherings, especially where there are people of different religious convictions.

There is no doubt that Catholics can have recourse to monasteries or to proven spiritual directors to receive assistance on their journey in the faith through personal prayer. But how many do that? The priest represents the obvious guide for most Catholics. Priests and bishops should learn to overcome shyness in this matter. It is not required that they should have arrived at the superior levels of mystical union with God before they can help their people to pray. They should, however, be men of prayer. And it is presumed that they have a good knowledge of the needed theology. Every priest or bishop can ask himself when it was that he last preached a homily to his people on how to engage in personal prayer.

Preparation is needed for personal prayer: recollection, silence, meditative reading of Holy Scripture or of suitable spiritual books, and a choice of a place for prayer. The ideal place is before Jesus in the tabernacle, but this is not always possible for everyone.

Liturgical prayer can help us very much with our personal prayer. Although we can make our prayer directly to the Father, or the Son, or the Holy Spirit, Christian prayer is generally Trinitarian: it is made to the Father, through the Son, in the unity of the Holy Spirit.

Our prayer should not be verbose, full of extravagant words. God has no need of our lecture. Jesus teaches us: "And in praying do not heap up empty phrases as the Gentiles do; for they think that they will be heard for their many words. Do not be like them, for your Father knows what you need before you ask him" (Mt 6:7–8). Elevation of the mind and heart to God is already prayer. "For me, prayer is a surge of the heart; it is a simple look turned toward heaven, it is a cry of recognition and of love, embracing both trial and joy."[2]

The priest should know what advice to give to a person who experiences distraction and aridity in prayer. But he should also discern when God is inviting a person to a higher level of prayer. It is said that the spiritual director of Saint Teresa of Avila retarded her life of prayer for several years with bad advice. He advised her to be more active in prayer, while God was elevating this elect soul to a form of union with him that was higher but less active.

The priest should encourage his people to compose ad hoc prayers for occasions such as the beginning or end of a meeting; before and after meals for a group of persons of differing religious affiliations; the blessing by parents over their children, especially when the children are going to undertake a journey or be absent from the family for some time; and moments of joy or sorrow for groups small and big. Obviously, liturgical prayers fixed by the Church to be conducted by her ministers have priority. But there is also

---

[2] Thérèse of Lisieux, *Manuscrits autobiographiques*, C 25r.

a place for personal, free compositions in situations that are neither official nor liturgical. Our Divine Master Jesus advised us always to pray and not to lose heart (cf. Lk 18:1).

Give us a priest or bishop who prays and who teaches his people to pray, and we can declare blessed that parish, that diocese!

THE EUCHARISTIC FAITH OF THE PRIEST

1. The Sacred Liturgy: The Role of the Priest and the Bishop

"The liturgy is the summit toward which the activity of the Church is directed; at the same time it is the font from which all her power flows."[1] It is Christ who associates with himself his Spouse, the Church, in the exercise of this sacerdotal function of his.[2] The sacred liturgy is the public worship of the Mystical Body of Jesus Christ, of the Head and members.[3] It therefore matters very much for the life of the Church how every liturgical action is celebrated.

It is clear that the sacred liturgy attains its highest solemnity when it is the Holy Father who celebrates. In the diocese, the Church manifests herself visibly when the diocesan bishop concelebrates the Eucharistic Sacrifice with his priests, with the assistance of deacons and minor ministers, and the participation of the people of God.[4]

But it is also a fact that for the majority of Catholics, the Holy Father and the diocesan bishop are somewhat distant. It is their parish priest or some other priest who is nearer to them. It is one of them that baptizes them, hears their confessions, celebrates Mass for them, preaches the homily,

[1] Vatican Council II, *Sacrosanctum Concilium* (December 4, 1963), 10.

[2] Cf. ibid., 7.

[3] Cf. Pius XII, *Mediator Dei* (November 20, 1947), 20.

[4] Cf. Vatican Council II, *Sacrosanctum Concilium*, 41.

blesses their marriage, and visits their sick. For them he prays the Liturgy of the Hours. And he dispenses to them the other blessings in the Church books.

The priest and the bishop should never forget that they are at the height of their vocation when they celebrate the sacred liturgy, especially the Holy Mass. Their *ars celebrandi* should be a contagious manifestation of the faith of the Church, a convincing sign of the personal faith of the priest, and a powerful catechesis that nourishes the people of God and sends them home on fire to live and share the inspiration received. It is sad to see a priest, or worse still a bishop, who rushes through a liturgical celebration with precipitous speed or conducts it without unction or without due preparation on his part, or on the part of his assistants at the altar.

Since the Eucharistic Sacrifice is "the fount and apex of the whole Christian life",[5] we shall begin with a meditation on the Eucharistic faith of the priest.

2. Priority of the Eucharist

The Eucharistic celebration is the memorial of the Passover mystery of Christ, the actualization and sacramental offering of his one sacrifice, in the liturgy of the Church that is his Body. "As often as the sacrifice of the cross in which Christ our Passover was sacrificed, is celebrated on the altar, the work of our redemption is carried on."[6] "The Eucharist is thus a sacrifice because it *re-presents* (makes present) the sacrifice of the cross, because it is its *memorial* and because it *applies* its fruit."[7]

---

[5] Vatican Council II, *Lumen Gentium* (November 21, 1964), 11.

[6] Ibid., 3.

[7] *CCC* 1366 (emphasis in original); cf. John Paul II, *Ecclesia de Eucharistia* (April 17, 2003), 12.

In the Holy Mass—the sacrifice of Christ, which becomes the sacrifice of the whole Church—Jesus invites us to his sacrificial banquet. It is the table of the Lord. In the Most Blessed Sacrament of the Eucharist is "contained truly, really, substantially the Body and the Blood of our Lord Jesus Christ, with the soul and divinity, and therefore the whole Christ".[8]

3. Union with Christ; the Mass Is Vertical

The Eucharistic Sacrifice is offered to the Father, with Christ, in the unity of the Holy Spirit. The Church learns to offer herself through Christ, with Christ, and in Christ.

The priest and the bishop must appreciate the importance of interior union with Christ especially during the celebration of Holy Mass. The active participation of all the baptized begins primarily with interior conversion of heart and union of the will with Christ.[9] Active participation is not activism, which creates confusion between the roles of the priest and the lay faithful.

Moments of silence and recollection during the celebration of Holy Mass—for example, before the Collect, after the Readings, after the homily, and after the reception of Holy Communion will help promote interior participation.[10] The celebrant should insist on this. And the choir should be helped to see why it should not fill every moment with yet another hymn.

Of help toward fostering the desirable interior sentiments are also the preparation of the priest with suitable prayers before Mass, together with thanksgiving after Holy Communion for all and thanksgiving on his own after Mass. The

---

[8] Council of Trent; DS 1651; cf. *CCC* 1374.

[9] Cf. Benedict XVI, *Sacramentum Caritatis* (February 22, 2007), 52, 53, 55.

[10] Cf. *General Instruction of the Roman Missal*, 54, 56, 66, 88.

Eucharistic Compendium, which is now near publication, will contain excellent prayers in this regard. During the day, the priest can prolong in a spiritual way the Mass he celebrated earlier whenever he feels the need to thank God, to praise him, to make reparation, or to request divine assistance in different activities of his ministry. In that way the Mass remains the center of his day.

It is not superfluous to add that the Mass is vertical, not horizontal, in direction. Jesus calls the liturgical assembly together so that we direct our worship and adoration to God. The people do not come to Mass for recreation, to watch a dance, or to admire the preacher. If they want entertainment, they know where to go: the theater, the cinema, or the parish hall! But when they are united in the liturgical assembly, the intention is to adore God, to praise him, to thank him, to ask pardon for their sins, and to make supplication for their many needs, spiritual and temporal.

4. The Beauty and the Majesty of the Mass

A Eucharistic celebration should be carried out with that beauty and majesty which strike all those who take part. The movements, full of unction, of the bishop or the priest and their assistants; the beauty, but at the same time, the seriousness, of the vestments; the artistic arrangement of the sanctuary in its simplicity; the manner of diction of the celebrant in the prayers, chants, admonition, and homily— all of these should help to manifest the great event that is the sacramental celebration of the paschal mystery of Christ. Every celebration of the Mass should be like a little vision of heaven.

The Servant of God Pope John Paul II testifies to this. He

speaks of Eucharistic celebrations he has held in big churches in Poland, in the Papal Basilica of Saint Peter in Vatican City, and in many other basilicas and churches around the world. Then he continues: "I have been able to celebrate Holy Mass in chapels built along mountain paths, on lakeshores and seacoasts; I have celebrated it on altars built in stadiums and in city squares. . . . This varied scenario of celebrations of the Eucharist has given me a powerful experience of its universal and, so to speak, cosmic character. Yes, cosmic! Because even when it is celebrated on the humble altar of a country church, the Eucharist is always in some way celebrated *on the altar of the world*."[11]

In the celebration of a beautiful liturgy, sacred music merits special mention. It is said that he who sings prays twice. If the hymns are theologically rich and artistically adequate, they will not fail to produce good fruit. Saint Augustine tells us how moved to tears he was when he listened to the execution of hymns and Psalms under the direction of Saint Ambrose in Milan. "How much I cried, listening to the accents of your hymns and canticles that resounded sweetly in your Church! A violent commotion: those accents flowed into my ears and distilled the truth in my heart, causing in me a warm sentiment of piety. The tears that flowed did me good."[12]

5. The Homily

In the homily, the people need to receive solid spiritual nourishment from their parish priest or bishop. The fruits of experience derived from years of kneeling or sitting before the Eucharistic Jesus and listening to him should be shared and

[11] *Ecclesia de Eucharistia*, 8 (emphasis in original).
[12] *Confessions* 9.6.14; cf. also Benedict XVI, *Sacramentum Caritatis*, 42.

put at the service of the flock in the homily. The sermon should be firmly based on the liturgical texts, Holy Scripture, and sound theology. This is neither the time nor the place for expressing one's opinions or making a sociological analysis. For the majority of the listeners, the homily is the best opportunity they have during the week to be nourished on the principles of the Catholic faith. Pope Benedict XVI has asked "ministers to preach in such a way that the homily closely relates the proclamation of the word of God to the sacramental celebration and the life of the community, so that the word of God truly becomes the Church's vital nourishment and support."[13]

For many major Church events, the bishop is the principal celebrant, and many of his priests concelebrate. The homily of the bishop should be a model. That is the best way for the bishop to persuade his priests to give to this ministry of the Word the importance that it deserves. The bishop could not remain indifferent if many of the homilies pronounced in his diocese were generally poor in quality, not nourished by Holy Scripture, theologically lacking, and going against the rules of pedagogy because they were too long and thereby tended to make some people sleep.

6. Adoration of the Eucharistic Jesus outside the Mass

We should thank Divine Providence that in many parts of the world Eucharistic adoration is increasing among the people of God. Adoration chapels are multiplying. The people pray for hours to Jesus exposed in the monstrance. Without paying any attention to human respect, some kneel, others stand, and yet others prostrate themselves.

[13] Benedict XVI, *Sacramentum Caritatis*, 46; cf. also *General Instruction of the Roman Missal*, 66; 2005 Synod of Bishops, prop. 19.

Such manifestations of faith are to be encouraged. The Sacrament of the Eucharist remains after Mass because Jesus is truly, really, and substantially present. It is logical that his people visit him to adore, praise, or thank him or simply to remain in his presence without engaging in words. Parishes or religious houses that have lost the practice of Eucharistic Benediction should be persuaded to take it up again, at least on Sundays and major solemnities. Eucharistic processions and congresses always witness the participation of a great many of the faithful. It would be sad if it were the clergy who doubted the readiness of the lay faithful to participate in these manifestations of faith. The priest should rather facilitate such expressions and thank God that his people are so fervent in the faith.

Eucharistic devotions outside Mass should not be seen as separated from the Eucharistic Sacrifice. They flow from the Mass and are not independent of it.

These devotions should also lead to a more intense communion with God and with one's neighbor. Jesus gives himself to us, and we should learn to give him to our brothers. The Holy Spirit urges us on to solidarity with others, in the different meanings of that concept. The Blessed Virgin Mary is for us a model. After the Archangel Gabriel brought her the divine message and she conceived the Son of God made man, the Virgin "went with haste" (Lk 1:39) to bring Jesus to John the Baptist, to Elizabeth, and to Zechariah. May the Most Blessed Virgin obtain for us the grace to live, with ever-growing authenticity, our faith in the Eucharist, both in the celebration of Holy Mass and outside that celebration.

XIII

THE DIVINE OFFICE
AND SACRAMENTALS

In addition to the sacraments, among which the Holy Eucharist is prominent, the sacred liturgy has two other components: the Liturgy of the Hours and sacramentals.

1. The Eminent Value of the Divine Office

The priest and bishop should give much attention to the Liturgy of the Hours. In fact, "by tradition going back to early Christian times, the divine office is devised so that the whole course of the day and night is made holy by the praises of God. . . . It is truly the voice of the bride addressed to her bridegroom; it is the very prayer which Christ Himself, together with His body, addresses to the Father."[1] The Church praises God and intercedes for the salvation of the whole world, not only by celebrating the Eucharist and the other sacraments, but also in other ways, such as through the Divine Office, which is the public prayer of the Church for the various hours of the day and night.

A priest or bishop who has such convictions will show great appreciation and love for the Liturgy of the Hours. The breviary should be his companion. He should pray the

---

[1] Vatican Council II, *Sacrosanctum Concilium* (December 4, 1963), 84.

different hours at their proper times as far as possible. There is no better place than before the Most Blessed Sacrament.

The bishop will associate with himself in this prayer of the Church his priest secretary and other clerics who perhaps live or work at the diocesan center. The Second Vatican Council wishes that priests who live in community, or who come together, even if they are not bound to pray the Office in choir, should pray together at least some part of the Liturgy of the Hours.[2] The bishop would already be giving a good example if he prayed the Divine Office, not only with the priests who live and work with him, but also with the clerics or religious in parishes or institutes that he visits. Example convinces more than precepts.

2. Involving the Lay Faithful in the Liturgy of the Hours

Apart from clerics, consecrated people, and others who are bound to pray the Office daily, the Church desires that the lay faithful should not be left out. "Pastors of souls should see to it that the chief hours, especially Vespers, are celebrated in common in church on Sundays and the more solemn feasts. And the laity, too, are encouraged to recite the divine office, either with the priests, or among themselves, or even individually."[3] Lauds and Vespers "are the two hinges on which the daily office turns; hence they are to be considered as the chief hours and are to be celebrated as such."[4]

[2] Cf. ibid., 99.
[3] Ibid., 100; cf. also Pius XII, *Mediator Dei* (November 20, 1947), 158.
[4] Vatican Council II, *Sacrosanctum Concilium*, 89a.

A layperson who occupies a high executive function in a company said to me: "I began to pray Lauds and Vespers in the Jubilee Year 2000. I intended to do this only for that year. But at the end of the year, I found that I could no longer live and work without these daily prayers of the Divine Office. Now I love to pray them every day."

Dioceses, or better still, bishops' conferences, have the honor and also the responsibility to see that the lay faithful have the Liturgy of the Hours in the needed local language, with good and approved translations. Apart from the complete Office, there is also the possibility of just a one volume edition, maybe without the Office of Readings.

The 2008 Synod of Bishops expressed the wish that the faithful participate in the Liturgy of the Hours, especially at Lauds and Vespers, and that, where they do not already exist, simple forms of the Liturgy of the Hours be prepared.[5]

3. The Priest and Sacramentals

The use of sacramentals merits attention from the priest or bishop. "Holy Mother Church has, moreover, instituted sacramentals. These are sacred signs which bear a resemblance to the sacraments: they signify effects, particularly of a spiritual kind, which are obtained through the Church's intercession. By them men are disposed to receive the chief effect of the sacraments, and various occasions in life are rendered holy."[6]

Think, for example, of blessings of persons (like the blessing of an abbot or virgins, or the rite of religious profession,

[5] Prop. 19.
[6] Vatican Council II, *Sacrosanctum Concilium*, 60; cf. *CCC* 1667-70.

or the blessing of some ministers). There is also the dedication or blessing of a church or of an altar, of holy oils, and of sacred vestments. The Book of Blessings also contains blessings for houses, offices, agricultural implements, vehicles, and so forth.[7] "There is hardly any proper use of material things which cannot thus be directed toward the sanctification of men and the praise of God."[8]

The priest and bishop should not undervalue the administration and use of sacramentals. These prayers of the Church are privileged moments for the proclamation of the Word of God, for homilies that show how our everyday lives and the use of creatures are parts of our life of faith, and for catechesis adapted to each circumstance. Sacramentals help the Christian people to learn to pray and to give the use of every creature its proper place in the Catholic faith. If due importance is not given to sacramentals, there may be the temptation, for some Christians, to join sects or new religious movements, even to return to superstitious practices of pre-Christian religions. The cleric would be making a mistake if he thought that Christians who are more advanced culturally and intellectually have no need of holy water, medals, statues of the saints, or processions to their sanctuaries. These manifestations of popular piety are not dark or irrational elements of the practice of the Christian faith. They can help Christians, not only to express their faith, but also to reinforce it. As human beings, we have need of human expressions that are perceptible, not unlike what is found between friends or people in love. Saint Teresa of Avila said regarding the use of holy water: "I often experience that there is nothing the devils flee from more—

---

[7] Cf. *CCC* 1671–73.
[8] Vatican Council II, *Sacrosanctum Concilium*, 61.

without returning—than holy water."[9] God has created us as body and soul. The sacraments make use of material and tangible things; sacramentals follow this same road indicated by the Creator.

4. The Consecrated Hands of the Priest

At ordination the hands of the priest are anointed with chrism for the sanctification of the Christian people and the offering of sacrifice to God. With these consecrated hands the priest offers the Eucharistic Sacrifice, touches the Body of Christ, and gives the Body and Blood of the Lord to the communicants. With these consecrated hands the priest blesses the people and imposes hands on them to invoke the blessings of God on them.

Christian people are not wrong when they honor the hands of the priest and want to kiss them. They are guided by faith when they bow or genuflect in front of the bishop and kiss his ring. The people know that the bishop's ring is a sign of the link of the bishop with the diocese, or even with the Church, where the bishop is a figure of Christ, Spouse of his Mystical Body.

It would not be right for the priest or bishop to refuse these gestures. It would be worse if they considered such to be the behavior of people who lack culture. And it would be false humility to repulse such manifestations of genuine faith. Indeed, the believing people who honor the priest or bishop in these ways are rendering honor to Christ the Priest through the ordained minister of Christ. What would we

---

[9] Teresa of Avila, *The Book of Her Life*, chap. 31, no. 4, in *The Collected Works of Saint Teresa of Avila*, vol. 1 (Washington, D.C.: ICS Publications, 1987), 265.

say of the ass that the priest rode before the advent of motor cars to bring the Most Blessed Sacrament to the sick? The believing people genuflected at the approach, not of the ass, but of the Eucharistic Jesus. The ass had no right to stop the manifestation of the faith of the people that was being offered, not to it, but to Christ. Such thoughts can help the priest or bishop not to get embarrassed in front of such manifestations of people's faith. And he should certainly not become proud, because in that case he would be taking the honor to himself.

If some cleric takes offense at this use of the figure of the ass, then may I advise him to read the following sentiments of Saint Josemaría Escrivá:

> Jesus accepts to have as throne a poor animal. I do not know if it happens to you, but I do not feel humiliated to look on myself before the Lord as an ass: *I am like a little ass before you, I am always with you, because you have taken me by your right hand, you lead me by the halter.* Think a little of the characteristics of an ass, now that there are not many of them remaining. Do not think of the old and stubborn animal that offloads its rancor with kicks of betrayal but rather of the young ass, with ears extended like antennae, sparing in eating, tenacious in work, trotting happy and secure. There are hundreds of animals more presentable, more able, more cruel. But Christ, to present himself as king to the people who were applauding him, chose the ass.[10]

When the priest or bishop blesses the people, it is good that he impose hands on them, on the head for men and perhaps on the shoulders for women, according to what may be advisable in a culture. There is the temptation for priests and bishops to become too intellectualistic or perhaps cerebral and not to appreciate the fact that for many people physical

[10] *E Gesù che passa* (Milan: Ares, 1973), no. 181.

contact with an ordained minister is welcome. I have personally noticed this desire to receive an imposition of hands along with the formula of blessing, and not just in the case of seminarians, novices, and elderly women but also in the case of professors, politicians, soldiers, customs officials at the airport, and even Muslims and people of African traditional religion.

I would like to add that outside liturgical celebrations, it is not at all forbidden for the priest or bishop to formulate a blessing a little more abundant in words than those fixed in the liturgical books. In this way, he can cover special needs, much like the prayer of the faithful at Mass, and thus better satisfy the community before him.

Let us thank the Lord Jesus, who makes us instruments of the blessings that a merciful and magnanimous God wants to send down abundantly on his people. Let us listen to Saint Paul, who says to us: "Pray constantly, give thanks in all circumstances" (1 Thess 5:17–18).

XIV

KINGDOM OF JUSTICE, LOVE, AND PEACE

The priest is a follower of Christ, who worked the mystery of man's salvation. Having subjected all creatures to himself, Jesus offered to the divine majesty a Kingdom of justice, love, and peace.[1] But the heart of the priest or bishop is pained to see in the world many situations showing a lack of justice, love, and peace.

1. *In Developing Countries*

In some countries that have been recently liberated from colonial domination, rather difficult situations exist: there are "leaders" who have with time become intransigent; there is a siphoning of public funds that remains unpunished; and in some countries, political elections are not transparent. The exploitation of natural resources, especially petroleum, which should be used by the government for needed development, often attracts the greed of local people and their foreign collaborators, such that much of the funds end up in private back accounts. There are people who suffer from the degradation of the ecology in their area, such that there is growing poverty side by side with oil wells.

---

[1] Cf. *Roman Missal*, Preface of the solemnity of Christ the King.

Agriculture is not always encouraged with modern means, with the result that the young people flock to the big cities to seek work, which they do not find. One can imagine the many negative consequences. Importing food that could have been produced locally increases considerably the foreign debt of the country in question.

Corruption in public life goes on, not without the collaboration of foreigners, who facilitate the transfer of funds. Sometimes it is not clear if the former colonial power is part of the problem rather than part of the solution.

This picture of the negative elements should be complemented by the mention of real positive signs of development, such as political elections carried out in a transparent way and leading to the victory of the opposition and its accession to power without violence; improvement in the communications media; and progress in matters educational and medical.

What cannot be denied is that many people are suffering, and the Lord could repeat what he said in the Exodus: "I have seen the affliction of my people. . . . I know their sufferings" (Ex 3:7).

2. Nonmaterial Poverty

Poverty is not only material, as exists in developing countries. There are also forms of poverty that Pope Benedict XVI calls nonmaterial in his Message for the World Day of Peace, January 1, 2009. These forms of poverty are not direct and automatic consequences of material deprivation. The Holy Father says:

> In advanced wealthy societies, there is evidence of *marginalization*, as well as *affective, moral and spiritual poverty*, seen

in people whose interior lives are disoriented and who experience various forms of malaise despite their economic prosperity. . . . It remains true, however, that every form of externally imposed poverty has at its root a lack of respect for the transcendent dignity of the human person.[2]

3. Sins with Serious Social Dimensions

Against justice, love, and peace are directed in particular those sins that have serious social dimensions. Certainly, "in its true sense, sin is always an act of the person, because it is the free act of an individual person and not properly speaking of a group or community."[3] But it remains true that every sin has a social dimension because of human solidarity. "*Certain sins, moreover, constitute by their very object a direct assault on one's neighbour. Such sins in particular are known as social sins.*"[4] The *Compendium* lists some of them: sins against the rights of the human person, beginning with the right to life; sins against the physical integrity of a person; sins against the freedom of others, especially the freedom of religion; sins against the common good; and sins against relations with various human communities. The *Compendium*, quoting John Paul II's *Sollicitudo Rei Socialis*, mentions two attitudes at the root of many social sins: "on the one hand, the all-consuming desire for profit, and on the other, the thirst for power, with the intention of imposing one's will upon others".[5]

[2] Message for the World Day of Peace (January 1, 2009), 2.
[3] *Compendium of the Social Doctrine of the Church* (Washington, D.C.: United States Conference of Catholic Bishops, 2004), 117.
[4] Ibid., 118 (emphasis in original).
[5] *Sollicitudo Rei Socialis* (December 30, 1987), 37; *Compendium of the Social Doctrine of the Church*, 119.

We can specifically mention the following sins that inflict a wound on justice, love, and peace in today's world: offenses against life and human dignity in the field of bioethics and in the treatment of embryos; trafficking in and use of drugs; indiscriminate pollution of the environment; and social injustice, which makes the rich richer while progressively impoverishing the already poor.

4. The Compassion of Jesus

When confronted with so much injustice and lack of love in the world, the priest cannot remain indifferent. From Jesus he learns to be compassionate. When Jesus saw people tired and hungry, he said to his disciples: "I have compassion on the crowd, because they have been with me now three days, and have nothing to eat; and I am unwilling to send them away hungry, lest they faint on the way" (Mt 15:32). And the Lord performed the miracle of the multiplication of the loaves and fishes. The people ate so well that they wanted to make him king! But Jesus did not want this type of office (cf. Jn 6:15).

Jesus in his public life healed the sick, gave sight to the blind, raised the dead to life, gave hope and pardon to sinners, and liberated the possessed from the power of the devil. In the synagogue of Nazareth, he read to the people a passage from the prophet Isaiah that describes the signs of the arrival of the messianic era:

"The Spirit of the Lord is upon me,
because he has anointed me to preach good news to the poor.
He has sent me to proclaim release to the captives
and recovering of sight to the blind,
to set at liberty those who are oppressed,

to proclaim the acceptable year of the Lord." (Lk 4:18; see
  Is 61:1–2)

It is to be noted that Jesus attended not only to the material
needs of the people but also—and primarily—to their spiritual hunger and thirst. Saint Mark records: "As he landed
he saw a great throng, and he had compassion on them, because they were like sheep without a shepherd; and he began to teach them many things" (Mk 6:34). It is Jesus who
teaches us to seek fraternal reconciliation before making our
offerings at the altar (cf. Mt 5:23–24). He teaches us not to
be attached to the things of this world (cf. Mt 25–34; Lk
12:16–21), and he refuses to judge between two brothers
who are quarrelling over the division of the property left
them by their father (cf. Lk 12:13–15).

5. The Priest, Apostle of Solidarity

Following the example of his Master, the priest or bishop
will seek to promote justice, love, and peace, as far as lies
in his power. "You give them something to eat" (Lk 9:13),
Jesus said to his Apostles. "Faithful to this summons from
the Lord", writes Pope Benedict XVI, "the Christian community will never fail, then, to assure the entire human family of her support through gestures of creative solidarity, not
only by 'giving from one's surplus', but above all by 'a change
of life-styles, of models of production and consumption, and
of the established structures of power which today govern
societies'."[6]

Interdependence is a fact. We have need of our brethren,
and they have need of us. When interdependence is not just

[6] Message for the World Day of Peace, 15. The quoted phrases are from
John Paul II, *Centesimus Annus* (May 1, 1991), 58.

tolerated but is sincerely accepted and generously lived, then the virtue of solidarity is generated. It is another name for Christian charity. My brethren are my companions in the pilgrimage that is life on earth.

Some of our brothers have more needs than others. There are the sick, the handicapped, the orphans, the elderly, and the persons who feel alone. At the end of the Eucharistic celebration, we are sent to serve God and our neighbor. Is there in each parish council a committee for social services? Is it customary that someone, in the name of the parish priest and the parish council, visits the old and the sick who could not come to Sunday Mass, to render them some service? What does the parish do, under the direction of the parish priest, to show solidarity to immigrants, to the unemployed, to the imprisoned, and to families that are mourning the death of their dear ones?

"A Eucharist which does not pass over into the concrete practice of love is intrinsically fragmented", writes Pope Benedict.[7] And Pope John Paul II tells us that what we do for the needy is an indicator of the authenticity of our Eucharistic celebration.[8]

The priest will gain in credibility if his initiatives to promote justice and live solidarity are backed up by an evangelical lifestyle; by not overloading himself with excess baggage in the journey that is life; and by sharing his goods with the poor, with seminarians, and with needy candidates to the religious life. And he can do this not only now but also after death, by including these intentions in his will.

It is the duty of the priest to remind those who are richer

---

[7] *Deus Caritas Est* (December 25, 2005), 14.
[8] Cf. *Mane Nobiscum Domine* (October 7, 2004), 28.

(economically, or in talent, education, or social opportunity) to give generously to others.

May the Lord Jesus, King of justice, love, and peace, attract us and bring us along in his entourage.

XV

THE VOICE OF THE CHURCH

1. Jesus the Master

While inaugurating the Kingdom of God, Jesus taught the people. His voice is clear, not ambiguous; it is a voice of love and not of condemnation, of hope and not of desperation, of invitation to repentance and not of rejection of the sinner.

Jesus "began to do and teach" (Acts 1:1). He lost no opportunity to teach the people: at the banks of the Sea of Galilee, in the synagogues, on the mountain, in the boat and from the boat, in the temple, during journeys, while working miracles, during dinners, at the unjust proceeding before Pontius Pilate, and even from the Cross. To the Apostles, he delivered personal teaching right up to the moment of his Ascension back into heaven (cf. Acts 1:3).

Jesus "taught them as one who had authority, and not as their scribes" (Mt 7:29). In fact, Jesus was called Rabbi, Master (cf. Mk 9:5; 10:51; 11:21; 14:45; Lk 5:5; 8:24, 45; 9:33, 49; 17:13; Jude 1:4).

2. The Church Must Give Witness to Jesus

The voice of the Church should be the voice of Jesus that resounds in our times. Like the voice of John the Baptist,

123

the voice of the Church should prepare for the Lord the people who are awaiting his arrival. Sometimes this voice will sound as a voice that cries out in the wilderness to people distracted by the things of this world. This voice of the Church should bring to people the joy of the Nativity of Jesus the Savior. Pope Benedict XVI describes this mission thus: "The Apostle says that the grace of God has appeared 'for all'. I would say that this also reveals the mission of the Church and, in particular, that of the Successor of Peter and his collaborators: to help make the grace of God, the Redeemer, ever more visible to everyone and to bring salvation to all."[1]

Generally it will be the Magisterium of the Church, as exercised by the Holy Father and the bishops in union with him, that authoritatively proclaims the Catholic faith and the doctrine of the Church, the truth that saves. But for the majority of Catholics, it will be their parish priest or other priests from whom they will hear the voice of the Church. Here is a mission that is high, demanding, noble, and joyful. People expect to hear this voice of the Church also in matters touching justice, love, and peace. "But how are men to call upon him in whom they have not believed? And how are they to believe in him of whom they have never heard? And how are they to hear without a preacher? And how can men preach unless they are sent? As it is written, 'How beautiful are the feet of those who preach good news!'" (Rom 10:14-15).

---

[1] Christmas Message to Roman Curia, December 22, 2008, *L'Osservatore Romano*, weekly English edition, January 7, 2009, p. 10.

3. A Voice Awaited

Many people in the world take the Church seriously when she speaks. They listen, even if they do not always live what is taught by the Pope, the bishop, or the bishops' conference. The priest should strive to be in complete unity with the official voice of the Church. The people expect to hear from him, not his own opinion, but the doctrine and message of Jesus, who sent him (cf. Jn 7:16). In the homily and in the confessional, the people have the right to hear, not the opinion of the priest, but the voice of Christ and of the Church.

There are many other voices in the world that want to be heard: the press, the television, politics, and public opinion. Often, some of these voices have been compromised. The voice of the Church should remain authentic, dependable, constant, and clear.

4. The Voice That Announces Christ the King

Many people in the modern world see Jesus as Savior, Friend, and Brother. All of that is true. But Jesus is also Lord, King, and, at the end of time, also Judge. He will come again to judge the living and the dead (cf. Mt 25:31–46).[2]

The voice of the Church should not be silent on this truth. The sovereignty of Christ should be recognized in both private and public life. Human society comes from the creating hands of God. Human beings should live according to the will of God.

[2] Cf. Credo.

Jesus, who took on himself the pains and sorrows of humanity, especially on the Cross, loves us with a love that culminates in the offering of his life for us. "Come to me, all who labor and are heavy laden, and I will give you rest" (Mt 11:28). The Kingdom of Christ is a Kingdom of love, harmony, respect for the rights of others, and forgiveness. If the Church does not preach this sovereignty of Christ, who will preach it?

5. Truth in Charity

The Church should proclaim the truth in love (cf. Eph 4:15). Her message is the truth that saves. The priest or bishop should not change the Gospel message. He should not try to water down the demands of the Word of God according to economic conditions or public opinion. The voice of the Church should be a distinct and clear one that does not pay attention to political correctness. It should not try to tell the people what the people like to hear but only what the Lord says (cf. 1 Kings 22:13–23).

Saint Paul exhorted Timothy to fulfill his ministry faithfully: "I charge you in the presence of God and of Christ Jesus who is to judge the living and the dead, and by his appearing and his kingdom: preach the word, be urgent in season and out of season, convince, rebuke, and exhort, be unfailing in patience and in teaching" (2 Tim 4:1–2).

There is need for courage, the gift of fortitude that comes from the Holy Spirit, to proclaim well the Gospel, especially in situations of injustice. This courage cost John the Baptist his head. Generally, the priest or bishop is not in any immediate danger of getting his head cut off. But more often, he can fear criticism from the daily papers, the annoyance of so-

called high society, marginalization by the rich and powerful, and perhaps a leaner collection at the offertory! But not
for these reasons should he compromise the Gospel. Holy
Scripture and tradition, interpreted and handed on by the
Magisterium, offer us security in the truth, without equiv-
ocation. What the surgeon does could make the patient suffer for the moment, but the hope is for healing and consequent joy.

6. Limits of the Voice of the Church

Sometimes people expect from the Church what is not
within the mandate of the Church to give. For example,
Christ has not given his Church the mission to produce political or economic recipes to solve the problems of society.
"The just ordering of society and the State is a central responsibility of politics."[3] And it is the role of the state to
promote this justice. Pope Benedict XVI is very clear:

> The Church cannot and must not take upon herself the po-
> litical battle to bring about the most just society possible.
> She cannot and must not replace the State. Yet at the same
> time she cannot and must not remain on the sidelines in the
> fight for justice. She has to play her part through rational
> argument and she has to reawaken the spiritual energy with-
> out which justice, which always demands sacrifice, cannot
> prevail and prosper.[4]

The priest or bishop should not forget that the lay faithful
not only can, but sometimes should, get engaged in politics
as citizens. It is a field of apostolate specific to the laity. The

---

[3] Benedict XVI, *Deus Caritas est* (December 25, 2005), 28.
[4] Ibid.

lay faithful are in their own right protagonists in the evangelization of society at the political level. And they should evangelize not only the parliament, the senate, and the political parties but also the professional organizations, the educational institutions, and other associations of this type.

Let us pray that every priest, every bishop may be an authentic voice of the Church announcing the truth of salvation also as regards justice, love, and peace and that every member of the lay faithful may be a credible witness to Jesus in his specific area of apostolate.

XVI

THE MOTHER IN WHOM WE TRUST

1. Mother of the Redeemer

In the divine plan of salvation for all humanity, Divine Providence assigned a very special role to the Virgin of Nazareth. He made her all-holy, "full of grace" (Lk 1:28). At her acceptance of the divine plan, at her "Fiat", the mystery of the Incarnation of the Word of God took place. The Mother of the Redeemer, the Most Blessed Virgin was an associate of the Savior from the annunciation to the visitation, from the birth of Jesus to his presentation in the temple, from the flight into Egypt to the years in Nazareth, from the wedding at Cana to Calvary. And with the nascent Church, the Virgin Mary was in the midst of the Apostles on the day of Pentecost.

Jesus has chosen the Blessed Virgin Mary to participate in our redemption. And the Blessed Virgin will lead us to Jesus. In her hands we entrust the hoped-for fruits of this retreat. We pray her to obtain for each of us the light, the grace, of the Holy Spirit, so that each of us may see what the Lord wants of him at the conclusion of these exercises, including on the question of resolutions for the future.

2. Looking for God Alone

Reflecting on the theme of last Monday, we pray Mary most holy to obtain for us the grace of lives oriented completely toward God, God who lives in unapproachable light. Mary the Virgin knew how to reply: "Behold, I am the handmaid of the Lord; let it be to me according to your word" (Lk 1:37). May her disposition be ours also. May she who was conceived without sin help us all, poor sinners, to seek only God, to do penance, and to live always for righteousness (cf. 1 Pet 2:24).

3. Faith in Jesus Christ

The meditations on the second day of this retreat concentrated on Jesus Christ, the center of our faith and the One who gives a sense of direction to our life. The Blessed Virgin Mary could say with even greater truth and justification than Saint Paul: "For to me to live is Christ, and to die is gain" (Phil 1:21). "It is no longer I who live, but Christ who lives in me" (Gal 2:20). The life of the Blessed Virgin was entirely christocentric. She lived for Christ and with Christ. In her, "the obedience of faith" (cf. Rom 16:26) found its perfect realization.[1] "The Blessed Virgin advanced in her pilgrimage of faith, and faithfully persevered in her union with her Son unto the cross, where she stood, in keeping with the divine plan, grieving exceedingly with her only-begotten Son."[2]

It is remarkable that the great Marian sanctuaries—such as Lourdes, Guadalupe, Czestochowa, Fatima, Aparecida,

[1] Cf. John Paul II, *Redemptoris Mater* (March 25, 1987), 13.
[2] Vatican Council II, *Lumen Gentium* (November 21, 1964), 58.

Loreto—and also the lesser ones, are centers where Jesus is greatly honored with Eucharistic celebrations and processions, with adoration, with the sacrament of Penance administered the entire day, and with the readiness of the pilgrims to do penance and bear suffering with faith and patience. The Blessed Virgin Mary leads us to Jesus.

Let us pray the Virgin Mary, the one who believed (cf. Lk 1:45), to obtain for us an unshakable faith in Jesus, the Son of God and the one Savior for all humanity. Mary is the "Morning Star" that announces the arrival of the Rising Sun, the Sun of Justice, Jesus the Savior. May she bring us to Jesus, she who is the first to believe, who pronounced her "Fiat" (cf. Lk 1:38), and who obtained by her intercession the first recorded miracle of Jesus that "manifested his glory; and his disciples believed in him" (Jn 2:11). May there well up within us at the same time a great love for Holy Scripture, where we meet Jesus the Redeemer, who makes our hearts burn within us. As can be seen from the Magnificat, our Lady had a profound knowledge of Holy Scripture.

May the hoped-for fruits of the 2008 Synod of Bishops on the Word of God begin already to bloom in our hearts, and may the expected postsynodal apostolic exhortation bring many graces for the whole Church so that people receive, read, meditate on, and live the Word of God.

4. The Blessed Virgin and the Church

One could not reflect on the Church without meditating on the Mother of God, who is "intimately united with the Church. As Saint Ambrose taught, the Mother of God is a type of the Church in the order of faith, charity and perfect union with Christ."[3] The Council continues: "But while in the most holy Virgin the Church has already reached that perfection whereby she is without spot or wrinkle, the followers of Christ still strive to increase in holiness by conquering sin (cf. Eph 5:27). And so they turn their eyes to Mary who shines forth to the whole community of the elect as the model of virtues."[4]

The Church honors the Virgin Mary especially in the Advent liturgy and in Christmastide. Her major feasts are distributed throughout the rest of the liturgical year. In this way the "great things" (Lk 1:49) done for Mary by the Almighty are celebrated in the cycle of the year that commemorates the mysteries of Christ.

The Mother of God helps us to love the Church, the Mystical Body of her Son; to appreciate the honor of being members of this Body; to carry one another's burdens; and to do our part for the spread of the Gospel.

May the Most Blessed Virgin intercede for the Successor of Saint Peter and all the bishops in communion with him and obtain for them the joy to see an approaching reunion of Christians, especially Catholics and Orthodox; to see in the Church a growth in holiness, unity, love, and harmony; and to see the fire of that missionary zeal which takes steps to share faith in Christ with waiting millions each year.

5. Our Lady Helps Us to Pray

The Blessed Virgin Mary knew how to direct toward God the movements of her heart. She knew how to pray. When Elizabeth praised Mary, the Virgin gave praise to God in

[3] Ibid., 63.
[4] Ibid., 65.

the Magnificat, a magnificent elevation of the heart, based 100 percent on Holy Scripture. Pope John Paul II writes that "*Mary is a 'woman of the Eucharist' in her whole life.* The Church, which looks to Mary as a model, is also called to imitate her in her relationship with this most holy mystery."[5] And Pope Benedict XVI writes on the same point: "Every time we approach the Body and Blood of Christ in the eucharistic liturgy, we also turn to her who, by her complete fidelity, received Christ's sacrifice for the whole Church."[6]

Let us pray the Most Blessed Virgin Mary to intercede for us for a greater openness to the grace of God in our personal prayer; for more faith and devotion in the various liturgical celebrations, especially Holy Mass; and for continuous renewal through our participation in the Liturgy of the Hours.

We direct a special request to our Blessed Mother for all priests in the Church. The great hopes of the Church; the undertakings in the missionary apostolate; the graces that flow from the various liturgical celebrations, especially the Mass—all presuppose for their full realization that there be priests according to the Heart of Jesus, priests who pray. Priests are much nearer to the people than the Holy Father and the bishops. May the Blessed Virgin protect them and obtain for each of them joy, fidelity, and perseverance in their sacerdotal vocation and mission.

6. The Mother of Suffering Humanity

Millions of people in the world suffer because of injustice and a lack of respect for human rights. The Mother of Christ,

[5] *Ecclesia de Eucharistia* (April 17, 2003), 53 (emphasis in original).

[6] *Sacramentum Caritatis* (February 22, 2007), 33.

King of kings and Lord of lords, will not forget her children who are striving to see clearly how better to witness to Jesus in society today, how to see on the face of the sick, the immigrant, the homeless, the refugee, or any other suffering person, Christ himself, the Christ who has said: "Truly, I say to you, as you did it to one of the least of these my brethren, you did it to me" (Mt 25:40). The Virgin Mary will help the Church to be, and continue to be, an authentic and credible voice of Jesus in the world of today.

"Behold, your mother!" (Jn 19:27) Jesus said to John at that supreme moment from the Cross. As the beloved disciple, let us take this exceptional Mother into our home.

XVII

AT THE EVENING OF LIFE

The priest or bishop who follows Jesus knows that "here we have no lasting city, but we seek the city which is to come" (Heb 13:14). It is important to reflect on how he prepares himself for the twilight of life.

1. Indications of the End of Life

The Book of Ecclesiastes (Qoheleth) tells us that there is "a time to be born, and a time to die" (Eccles 3:2). There are several indications that announce that the conclusion of our earthly pilgrimage is not far off. Aches and pains begin. One begins to forget things more than before. One goes from one specialized doctor to another. Sometimes the doctors, in a delicate way, make the patient draw the conclusion that the physicians have done their best, but nature will run its course!

2. The Attitude of the Cleric

It matters very much what the attitude of the sick priest or bishop is in such circumstances. No doubt, he is free to hope to live a hundred years, considering all the advances made by modern medicine. But would it not be more realistic to put before him the consideration that every generation has registered a 100 percent mortality rate?

What type of homily does the priest or bishop preach to his people from the hospital or the wheelchair? Someone has remarked that Pope John Paul II taught us more from his wheelchair than from his fourteen encyclical letters. This is a way of underlining his complete acceptance of the will of God, which came to him by way of so many hospitalizations and surgical interventions, and difficulty in walking and even in speaking. He lived personally his apostolic letter *Salvifici Doloris* of February 11, 1984. The Letter to the Hebrews advises us: "Remember your leaders, those who spoke to you the word of God; consider the outcome of their life, and imitate their faith" (Heb 13:7).

While we are still in good health, we could put some questions to ourselves: If I, a priest or bishop, were in the future to be sick for a protracted length of time, what would be the better thing for me to do for the good of the parish or the diocese? Does there not come a time when a person who has served God and the Church for many years, and now is not in good health, should request to have lifted from him the chief responsibilities he has held, in order to permit another cleric in better health to steer the boat and also to allow the sick person more tranquility to pack his bags and prepare to meet his Creator? Certainly, the persons near the sick bishop or parish priest will hesitate to pronounce the word *resignation*, lest they appear to be ungrateful. But should it not be the sick person who first raises the question, taking into account that the *Code of Canon Law* deliberately closes with canon 1752, which advises that it should always be borne in mind that in the Church the salvation of souls must always be the supreme law?

3. The Death of a Christian

It is not superfluous to remind the priest or bishop what death for a Christian should be. Such a consideration can help him to live with greater serenity the final moments of his life on earth.

The Christian lives in Christ and dies in him. "Blessed are the dead who from now on die in the Lord. Blessed indeed, says the Spirit, that they may rest from their labors, for their deeds follow them" (Rev 14:13). "For to me to live is Christ, and to die is gain" (Phil 1:21), says Saint Paul. Saint Peter shows great serenity at the thought of the fact that death is not far away, but at the same time he does not forget the people entrusted to him. He wrote them: "I know that the putting off of my body will be soon, as our Lord Jesus Christ showed me. And I will see to it that after my departure you may be able at any time to recall these things" (2 Pet 1:14–15).

The death of a Christian has great value when the person has lived in union with Christ. Moreover, death teaches us all, in a rather drastic way, that we must leave everything (cf. Mt 19:27) and follow Jesus. A believer can, and should, strive to live this truth all the years of his earthly pilgrimage.

Christian life is a life of hope. Eternal life is "like plunging into the ocean of infinite love".[1] Jesus reassures us: "I will see you again and your hearts will rejoice, and no one will take your joy from you" (Jn 16:22). At death, the Christian leaves behind everything on earth, but then he finds God, and, finding him, he has eternal life.

---

[1] Benedict XVI, *Spe Salvi* (November 30, 2007), 12.

4. Material Preparations

From the point of view of material preparations for the evening of life, the priest or bishop could ask himself what he has done to help and encourage his possible successors. Are the files in the office in good order? Has his will been written and brought up to date? Is there included in the will a provision for the poor, the seminarians, and the candidates to the consecrated life who need financial help? Has he indicated clearly where his vestments, other altar equipment, and books should go? Has the sick cleric forgotten to set aside some money for Mass intentions for his own eternal repose?

Even if these appear to be material preoccupations, it is better to think of them when one is still in good health.

5. The Sacred Liturgy Accompanies Us

As the sacred liturgy gives us birth in the waters of Baptism at the beginning of our Christian life, so it accompanies us at such moments as the time of sickness at home or in the hospital, at the critical moment of death, and to the grave and beyond.

The *Roman Missal* contains beautiful Masses for the sick, the dying, and the dead. In celebrating the sacrament of Anointing of the Sick, the priest or bishop prays for the recovery of the sick person if it is God's will, for the remission of sins, and for a holy death if Divine Providence so disposes. The prayers for the dying in the *Roman Ritual* are of great comfort both to the sick and to their relatives. The

Office for the Dead in the Liturgy of the Hours is a rich and instructive prayer.

Considering that it is priests and bishops who preach to the people about the meaning of our life on earth, and that it is they who administer the sacraments to the sick and bury the dead, should these clerics then not be model Christians who live on earth like pilgrims who are going to their eternal home? Should they not recite with faith Psalm 122: "I was glad when they said to me, 'Let us go to the house of the LORD'"? Indeed, they pray: "Holy Mary, Mother of God, pray for us sinners now and at the hour of our death. Amen."

We conclude with the Collect of the Mass of this day, Saturday in the First Week of Lent: "O God, Father of eternal mercy, grant that our hearts may be converted to you, so that in seeking the one good necessary and in works of brotherly love, we may always be consecrated to your praise." Amen.[2]

[2] Here the author is translating from the Latin. We give his translation, rather than the ICEL translation.—ED.

ADDRESS OF HIS HOLINESS BENEDICT XVI
TO THE ROMAN CURIA AT THE CONCLUSION
OF THE WEEK OF SPIRITUAL EXERCISES

Redemptoris Mater Chapel
Saturday, March 7, 2009

Your Eminence,
Dear Venerable Confreres,

To say "thank you" is one of the Pope's most beautiful duties. I would like here, on behalf of all of us and all of you, to express heartfelt thanks to you, Your Eminence, for these meditations which you have given us. You have guided us, illumined us and helped us to renew our priesthood. Your talks were no theological acrobatics. Instead of theological acrobatics, you offered us a healthy doctrine, the good bread of our faith.

In listening to your words, I remembered a prophecy of the Prophet Ezekiel interpreted by Saint Augustine. In the Book of Ezekiel, the Lord, God as a Shepherd, says to his people: I will lead my sheep to the mountains of Israel, to good pastures. And St. Augustine asks where these mountains of Israel are to be found and what these good pastures mean. He replies: the mountains of Israel and the good pastures are Sacred Scripture, the word of God which gives us true nourishment.

Your preaching was steeped in Sacred Scripture, showing great familiarity with the word of God, interpreted in the context of the living Church, from the Fathers to the *Catechism of the Catholic Church* and always within the context of the Reading and the Liturgy. And precisely in this way, Scripture was made present with its full timeliness. Your theology, as we have said, was not abstract theology but marked with healthy realism. I admired and enjoyed this practical experience of your fifty years of priesthood, of which you spoke and in the light of which you helped us to actualize our faith. You spoke to us words that are right and practical for our life, our conduct as priests, and I hope that many people will also read these words and take them to heart.

At the start, you began with this ever fascinating and beautiful account of the first disciples who followed Jesus. Still somewhat hesitant and timid they ask: Rabbi, where are you staying? And the answer, which you interpreted, is "Come and see". In order to see we must come, we must walk after, we must follow Jesus, who always goes before us. Only by walking after and following Jesus can we see too. You have shown us where Jesus dwells, where his dwelling place is: in his Church, in his word, in the Blessed Sacrament.

Thank you, Your Eminence, for your guidance. Let us all continue on the way towards Easter with a new impetus and with new joy. I wish you all a good Lenten Season and a happy Easter.

To Our Venerable Brother
CARDINAL FRANCIS ARINZE,
Prefect Emeritus of the
Congregation for Divine Worship
and the Discipline of the Sacraments

Spiritual Exercises always constitute, in the life of the Christian, a special moment of grace, for which to be particularly grateful to the Lord. This is the sentiment that I also carry in my heart, at the end of the days of retreat at the beginning of Lent, in which you, dear Cardinal, have preached to me and to my collaborators in the Roman Curia meditations that we have appreciated. Therefore, while I give fervent thanks to God, I want at the same time to express deep gratitude to you, because you have dispensed God's word with wisdom and fidelity and with generous disponibility.

You, dear Cardinal, have organized the spiritual journey according to a thematic order inspired by the priestly vocation, modeled naturally on that of the first disciples of Christ. The starting point, in fact, was the call given by the Lord to his first followers. From there, you have guided us to revisit, almost as in a type of "spiritual seminary", the great themes of the Christian life: sin and conversion; the paschal mystery, center of all the Scriptures; Church communion and mission; prayer and the Eucharist; pastoral charity; the maternity of the Virgin Mary; and the heavenly fatherland.

Commenting on the biblical texts, venerable Brother, you have communicated to us, with the gracefulness and the depth that we associate with you, the fruit of your personal experience of life and of your priestly ministry, of which you recently celebrated the fiftieth anniversary. In this way, with the authority that comes from personal experience, you have helped us to rediscover and deepen the primacy of the presence of Christ in our lives: Christ met, Christ followed and always again to be followed, inexhaustible source of joy and peace.

All of this has an inestimable value, and only God can fully thank you and adequately reward you. For my part, dear Cardinal, I assure you of frequent remembrance in my prayer, for all your intentions, while from my heart I give you a special Apostolic Blessing, which I happily extend to all your dear ones.

From the Vatican,
March 7, 2009

BENEDICT XVI, Pope